Dreamers & **Doers**

Unveiling the Power of Hope, Hustle, and Transformation

By

Jeffrey Nelson Cole

"See a dream like a mastery"

"The art of mastery determines the dreamers and doers"

By
Jeffrey Nelson Cole

Table of Contents

Introduction

Have you ever thought about whether your dreams could actually come true? What if turning dreams into reality was less of a challenge and more of a journey filled with hope, hard work, and transformation? What propels a dream from a mere wish to something tangible? Perhaps it is that inner voice of hope encouraging dreamers to take the plunge and aim higher.

I believe that *when our hearts carry twin flames of hope and hustle,* nothing can stop us from turning our dreams into reality. Our vision and actions are the two pieces of the puzzle that together create the power of transformation. Just as wishful thinking is futile without actionable planning, hustle without a vision and purpose is also useless. This book is all about the trio of the three "Hope, Hustle, and Transformation." It is a pyramid with hope at its foundation, hustle in the middle that leads to the peak- *the transformation.*

Through the ebbs and flows of my own journey, I discovered that dreams are the celestial architects of our aspirations, the stars that guide our vision. They are born in the quiet moments of contemplation, where the mind, free from the constraints of reality, dares to soar into the limitless expanse of possibilities. Actions are the gravitational forces that pull these dreams into the orbit of reality. They are the tangible steps, the deliberate movements that bridge the gap between the abstract and the concrete. The thing that we all need to understand is that we need to align our dreams with actions to achieve fruitful results.

Working as a financial specialist, there is one thing that I always tell my clients: *"Dreams don't work unless you do,"* and that is exactly what I learned through the challenges I faced over the years. Back in Monrovia, when I was a young boy, all I had was a dream, and I saw myself as someone crunching numbers and mastering the art of finances, just as my uncle did. But my dream could not have seen the light of day if I hadn't followed the long-twisted road of hustle. Coming to Texas with a suitcase in one hand and a scholarship in another, the only thing that kept me going was my unwavering resolve and the hunger to gain financial literacy. Through this journey, I learned the importance of perseverance and determination in achieving new heights of success.

While learning about finance, I saw beyond the numbers; I saw a world where financial wisdom was not a privilege reserved for a select few but a beacon that could guide anyone willing to learn and work hard. My story is not just about balancing ledgers and memorizing formulas but breaking barriers, challenging the notion that finance is a tapestry woven exclusively by the privileged. For me, every challenge is an opportunity, every obstacle a stepping stone on the path to a vision only I can perceive clearly.

Inspired by my personal experiences and those of others, one key lesson that I kept with me all those years is that having financial knowledge and wisdom fuels your hopes and helps you hustle in the right direction. That is why I wanted to become a financial specialist and guide people in the right direction by providing them with necessary financial guidance. The idea for this book is also sourced from the same context, that is, to share the stories of hope, hustle, and transformation with you all, so no matter how big or small your dreams are, you end up achieving them and hope for more.

This is not just a book; it is a guide for those who want to bring their dreams to life, work hard with a purpose, and go through a change that goes beyond the usual. As you read on, you will discover what makes a person a dreamer or a doer and how your dreams can shape your life. We will also look into the changing financial landscape of the world, how employment has transformed over the years, and how traditional careers are morphing into entrepreneurship. Today, the world belongs to those who dream of bringing ideas to life and that entrepreneurial spirit is pivotal to modern age success. The job market has also evolved where upskilling and reskilling are crucial to climb up the ladder. Therefore, in chapters 3 and 4 of this book, I have specifically focused on providing detailed insights regarding the shift you would like to take from employment to entrepreneurship and how to find the right business for you.

The path that follows is all about believing in yourself, staying determined, and not giving up in the face of failures. Without courage, confidence, and the mindset to see failures as opportunities, I would not have made it this far, and I would like to say the same for everyone who dreams! There are going to be great challenges that might come your way, and it often feels like you don't have what it takes to achieve your goal, but with self-belief as your armor and perseverance as the weapon, you get to swim through the turbulent waters.

Chapter 1

The Dreamers and Doers

"Are you a dreamer or a doer?" This one sentence has made me strive through some of the most challenging and testing times of my life. My uncle was a firm believer in "Dreams don't work unless you do," so every time I had a discussion about my career and life journey with him, he reminded me of the importance of finding the right amount of courage to act on what I dream. After working as a financial specialist for the most part of my life and dealing with all sorts of people, I have realized that dreams and actions represent the two sides of the same picture, the two ends of one rope, and the synergy of both can do wonders in this world. Without dreams, you cannot think of the unthinkable, and without action, the thoughts can never culminate into reality. So, they both are the yin and yang that together build a successful life.

Life teaches us all differently, and based on our experiences, we develop different perspectives and approaches to life. That is how dreamers and doers are born; we all are pretty much the same, but it is our values, fears, and vision that shape our behavior. So, in this chapter, we will not only understand what makes a doer different from a dreamer but also about why such difference matters in life?

Who Are the Dreamers and the Doers?

To explain the inherent differences between a dreamer and a doer, let me draw a comparison between two of my clients, Alex and Taylor.

They are both ambitious individuals with big aspirations, but their approaches to achieving their goals are as distinct as night and day. Alex is the quintessential dreamer. He has a head full of grand ideas, a notebook filled with sketches of his future success, and a heart fueled by passion. Alex spends hours daydreaming about what could be, envisioning a life of success, recognition, and fulfillment. Every conversation with Alex is sprinkled with phrases like "someday," "imagine if," and "what if I could..." The world of possibilities is Alex's playground, and they thrive in the realm of creativity and boundless potential. Alex is an aspiring writer. He has a drawer full of unfinished novels, each beginning with a burst of inspiration but never reaching completion. Alex spends hours discussing plot twists, character arcs, and the profound themes of their stories with friends. Their dream is to be a celebrated author, but Alex often gets lost in the romance of writing without putting in the consistent effort needed to finish a manuscript.

On the other hand, there is Taylor. Taylor is the embodiment of action. He believes in turning dreams into reality through hard work, determination, and a relentless pursuit of his goals. While Dreamers are lost in the beauty of what could be, Doers like Taylor are busy making things happen in the here and now. Taylor is all about setting specific, achievable targets, creating detailed plans, and then rolling up their sleeves to get the job done. "Why wait?" is Taylor's motto, and every moment is an opportunity to make progress.

Taylor also dreams of becoming a writer. However, Taylor sets specific goals, like writing a certain number of words each day. He attends writing workshops, seeks feedback, and submits his work to publishers. Taylor understands that success in writing requires not just dreams but a dedicated commitment to the craft. While his progress may be incremental, Taylor is steadily moving closer to their goal.

In essence, dreamers like Alex bring imagination and vision to the table, painting the picture of what could be. Doers like Taylor, on the other hand, add the brushstrokes of action, turning those dreams into tangible achievements. Both have their place in the journey of success, but it is often the combination of dreaming and doing that leads to the most fulfilling outcomes. From the examples of Alex and Taylor, here are some differences between dreams and doers that we can learn:

- *Talkers vs. Workers*: Dreamers are the poets of their dreams, spinning tales of inspiring visions that can leave you in awe. On the flip side, doers are a bit more tight-lipped. They believe in action rather than excessive chatter. While dreamers talk, doers work tirelessly, making sacrifices and pushing forward.

- *Postponing vs. Starting*: Dreamers have a knack for finding reasons to delay their dreams. Ask them, and they might give you a laundry list of justifications for not starting today. Doers, however, are a different breed. They set deadlines, and if they are ready, they start right away – sometimes even before they feel fully prepared.

- *Speculation vs. Experimentation*: Dreamers can get lost in a world of speculation, meticulously planning for every possible scenario. Meanwhile, doers believe in getting their hands dirty through experimentation. They understand that doing something is the best way to figure out what works and what doesn't. They embrace failure, fix what's broken, and keep improving.

- ***Excuses vs. Action:*** When things don't go as planned, dreamers often resort to finding excuses and might even hit the pause button. Doers, however, are solution-oriented. They confront problems head-on, continuously seeking new solutions to overcome hurdles.

- ***Listening to Fear vs. Working Through Fear:*** Fear is an inevitable companion whenever you go on something new. Dreamers might let fear paralyze them, contemplating the 'what ifs.' Doers, on the other hand, find ways to push past the limits of their fears. They acknowledge fear's presence but let it fuel their determination rather than hinder it.

- ***Stopping vs. Being Inspired by Failure:*** Failure can be a dream crusher for dreamers. One setback and they might call it quits on their aspirations. Doers, however, view failure as a friend, a guide helping them improve and evolve. They don't stop with failure; they are inspired by it to keep pushing their boundaries.

- ***Losing Interest vs. Cultivating Curiosity:*** Dreamers can be like butterflies, fluttering from one dream to another, losing interest quickly. Doers, in contrast, cultivate curiosity. They are perpetual learners, always eager to acquire knowledge and grow. Bill Gates, in 2019, emphasized the pivotal role of curiosity in learning, stressing its critical importance in the ever-evolving landscape of knowledge acquisition.

Dreamers, fueled by hope, envision possibilities and set ambitious aspirations. Their dreams become the beacon that guides their journey. However, the transformative magic happens when hope converges with hustle—the relentless, determined effort to turn dreams into reality. Doers embody the essence of hustle; they take decisive actions, overcome challenges, and persistently work toward their objectives. Hope provides the vision, while hustle translates that vision into tangible progress. In this symbiotic relationship, hope infuses the journey with optimism, and hustle propels it forward with concrete, deliberate actions. Together, hope and hustle form a powerful alliance, propelling dreamers and doers alike toward the fulfillment of their aspirations.

The Intersection of Hope and Hustle

"Hope is not a strategy, but strategies are built on hope."

- Rudy Giuliani

In the intersection of hope and hustle, people find the delicate balance between optimism and proactive effort. It is the sweet spot where belief in a better future meets the relentless determination to make it happen. Hope is the spark that ignites the journey. It is the belief that despite challenges, a brighter tomorrow is within reach. Hustle, on the other hand, is the unwavering commitment to translating hope into reality. Consider James, a startup founder. James doesn't just dream of revolutionizing an industry; he's in the trenches daily, networking, iterating, and putting in the hard work required to turn his vision into a thriving business. In this intersection, hope provides the vision, while hustle fuels the journey. Let's understand what happens when you sync the two!

Strategic Optimism

I had a client named Mr. Anderson, who had invested a significant portion of his portfolio in industries that were particularly susceptible to economic downturns. When the market took a hit during a recession, his investments suffered considerable losses. Mr. Anderson, understandably, was anxious and considering drastic measures like pulling out of the market altogether. Instead of succumbing to the prevailing panic, I asked him to employ a strategy grounded in strategic optimism. In our discussions, I acknowledged the present challenges but emphasized the potential for recovery and growth in the future. I presented a detailed analysis of the market, highlighting historical patterns of resilience after downturns.

Together, we recalibrated his portfolio, strategically diversifying investments to mitigate risks while identifying sectors poised for future growth. It was a meticulous process, combining realism about the current market conditions with a hopeful outlook for the long term. As the market gradually stabilized and then rebounded, Mr. Anderson's portfolio not only recovered its losses but also began to show impressive gains. The strategic optimism we embraced during the downturn had not only preserved his wealth but had strategically positioned him to benefit from the eventual market upswing.

So, what is strategic optimism? It is the art of balancing realism with a hopeful mindset. Individuals at the intersection of hope and hustle acknowledge the challenges ahead but choose to believe in the potential for positive outcomes. It is a conscious decision to view obstacles as opportunities, leveraging optimism as a strategic tool in their journey.

Resilience: Bouncing Back

In this dynamic space, resilience takes center stage. Those standing at this intersection understand that setbacks are not roadblocks but rather integral parts of their journey. Hope acts as a resilient cushion, allowing us to bounce back from failures. Each stumble becomes a learning opportunity and we adapt with every experience, reinforcing our commitment to the path ahead. Recalling one of the most profound experiences of my life during the Ebola outbreak in Dallas, Texas, in 2014, I found myself among the direct victims of this relentless virus. As the CDC confirmed the severity of my symptoms, I, along with three others, was mandated to be quarantined for the safety of the public. We became, in a way, perceived threats to the community's health.

After spending a few anxious days in our residence, the CDC and the city of Dallas decided to relocate us far from the city. The fear and threat from our neighbors were palpable due to our encounter with Ebola symptoms. The entire nation was on edge, with the global media seeking updates on our condition. The CDC assigned diligent doctors and compassionate social workers to check on us daily. We were instructed to monitor our health three times a day, recording our temperatures to present to the social workers during their visits.

During the quarantine, we received essential donations like food, clothing, gadgets for the little ones, and personal computers to keep us engaged. It was an unnerving experience, but the CDC anticipated that at least one of us would display symptoms. Miraculously, all four of us completed the 21-day quarantine without any issues.

However, our freedom was still restricted even after the quarantine ended. Under CDC guidelines, we were under supervision and limited gatherings. Despite losing all my belongings, which were required to be destroyed to contain the spread of the disease, I considered it a heartbreaking event but found solace in being alive. I chose not to expose my experience on social media or engage with journalists, allowing me to reclaim my life swiftly. This experience, to me, symbolizes a story of hope, resilience, and transformation amidst the Ebola outbreak. Being a direct victim, I faced unimaginable challenges, but the ordeal became a testament to the strength of the human spirit to endure and emerge stronger in the face of adversity. Sharing my story is not just a personal revelation but a way to inspire others facing hardships, demonstrating that even in the darkest times, there is a remarkable capacity within us to overcome.

Purposeful Action: Aligning Effort with Hopeful Vision

The intersection of hope and hustle is characterized by purposeful, directed action. It is not merely about working hard; it is about aligning every effort with a vision deeply rooted in hope. Each action is intentional, contributing to the realization of a greater purpose. Hope fuels our drive, giving us a sense of direction in our endeavors. In the world of finance, where market fluctuations can evoke uncertainty, every move becomes a calculated step toward a greater purpose.

Let's go back to Mr. Anderson's story! In the face of market downturns, Mr. Anderson's initial response was natural – a sense of anxiety and a contemplation of drastic measures. However, instead of succumbing to panic, we charted a course that aligned with a vision deeply rooted in hope – the hope for the recovery and growth of his investments. The intentional steps involved a meticulous analysis of market conditions, a strategic diversification of his portfolio, and a thoughtful identification of sectors poised for future growth. Each action was not a random reaction to market fluctuations but a purposeful move contributing to the realization of greater financial stability.

How Dreams Initiate Transformation?

As my mother used to say, **"Our lives are like the Liberian quilts; we make patches of joy, sorrow, and survival, sewn together with the thread of our will."**

From her, I learned the importance of "will" and how figments of our imagination set a cycle of ultimate transformation in our lives. However, it does take time and consistent efforts to enjoy the fruits of our dreams. I have witnessed the transformation of countless lives, seen the light return to eyes clouded by financial worries, and felt the joy of people realizing the potential within them. Every transformative journey begins with a dream – a vision of what could be, an aspiration that transcends the present. A few years back, I met a client named Sarah. She is a successful entrepreneur now. Sarah envisioned a world where sustainable and eco-friendly products were not just a niche but a mainstream choice for consumers. Her dream was to create an empire built on the values of environmental responsibility and ethical business practices. Sarah's dream prompted her to defy conventional career paths. Instead of settling for a traditional job, she decided to channel her passion into entrepreneurship. The dream acted as a catalyst, propelling her into uncharted territories, driven by the belief that her vision could reshape an industry.

As with any transformative journey, Sarah encountered challenges. Limited resources, skepticism from industry veterans, and the complexities of establishing a business from scratch were hurdles she had to navigate. However, the dream acted as a resilient force, pushing her to find innovative solutions, seek mentorship, and persevere through the tough times.

Sarah's dream required a continuous process of learning and adaptation. In order to make her mark in the eco-friendly product market, she educated herself about sustainable practices, stayed abreast of industry trends, and embraced a mindset of continuous improvement. The dream was not just a destination but a guiding star for ongoing growth. As Sarah's venture began to take shape, her dream became a rallying point for a team that shared her vision. The dream initiated a collective transformation, aligning individuals towards a common purpose. It wasn't just Sarah's dream anymore; it became a shared aspiration that fueled the entire team's commitment and dedication.

Sarah's dream didn't just transform her life; it had a ripple effect on the industry. Her eco-friendly products gained traction, influencing consumer preferences and challenging established norms. The dream now materialized into a successful business and became a driving force for positive change within the industry.

That is how one single dream can initiate the cycle of transformation. If you are passionate enough, that single idea can into a reality. Now, take a moment to reflect on your dreams. What ignites your passion? What keeps you awake at night with excitement? Identify those dreams and write them down on a passion map. Putting down your ideas on a tangible piece of paper lets you focus and helps you plan your moves. Next, draw inspiration from your own challenges, just as I did. Understand that setbacks are not roadblocks but opportunities to grow and learn. Let your dreams be the driving force that propels you forward, even in the face of adversity. Lastly, commit to your hustle. It is true that dreams initiate transformation, but it is the daily grind, the dedication to your craft, that brings them to life.

Why do people choose little goals? In answering this question, let us first consider self-doubt; many people fail to believe in themselves that they can complete any task easily without a helper. So, for that reason, they are very afraid to fail. One of the main reasons people consider little goals is that they are afraid of failure. For that reason, they ideally imprison their mind and that of their soul, believing that they cannot break even. So, it is important to first program our mind and brain with success but not only that, we should also back it up with quality of work and effort in making sure that we are working toward a good cause. As a Dreamer, we can only make it if our minds are rich with positivity, knowing fully well that everything is possible only if our mind is set on greatness. We need to believe in ourselves and free our minds and soul from any imprisonment that we might think of. Again, we should not consider ourselves that we can solve all problems. This type of belief hides our ways of life as a dreamer. We should always give ourselves a chance to observe any situation around us, as some may have different meanings, and they also add to our journey of life as a doer. Having a bigger goal helps us to strive harder as this process allows us to think out of the box. Helping us to feel uncomfortable in a sense that pushes us out of our comfort zone. A bigger goal is a bigger dream. And it is good for us, the dreamers, to understand ways in which we can program our minds as a positive thinker.

Determining Your Dream Job

Choosing a job that aligns with your passions is akin to discovering a hidden reservoir of boundless energy. It transforms the daily grind into a meaningful pursuit, where each task becomes a step toward personal fulfillment. A job that resonates with your values and interests not only brings satisfaction but also fuels long-term commitment. The sense of purpose derived from your work becomes the driving force behind your professional journey. Your job is not just a means of earning; it is a platform for growth. When you choose a role that challenges and nurtures your skills, you step on a continuous journey of self-improvement, evolving both personally and professionally.

How to Determine Your Ideal Job?

All great things begin with introspection. What are your passions? What activities make you lose track of time? Reflect on your values, skills, and interests. This process lays the foundation for understanding your ideal career path. Don't be afraid to explore various fields. I, too, ventured into different roles before finding my niche. Whether through internships, volunteering, or part-time jobs, each experience is a stepping stone toward clarity. The next important step is to connect with professionals in different industries. Seek their insights, understand their journeys, and learn from their experiences. Networking not only broadens your horizons but also provides valuable perspectives on potential career paths.

In my own journey, I initially pursued a conventional career path that seemed secure but lacked passion. It was only when I took a leap into a field that resonated with my interests - in my case, financial consulting - that I truly felt a sense of purpose. The challenges I faced were opportunities for growth and the satisfaction derived from helping others navigate their financial landscapes fueled my commitment to the profession.

I had to undergo a process of self-discovery, trying different roles and even facing moments of uncertainty. However, each experience contributed to the clarity I needed to determine my ideal job. The journey, with its twists and turns, ultimately led to a fulfilling career that goes beyond a paycheck—it is a daily expression of my values and aspirations.

Determining your job is a profound act of self-investment. It is about aligning your professional life with your innermost passions and values. Through self-reflection, exploration, and networking, you can uncover the ideal job that not only provides financial stability but also becomes a source of genuine satisfaction and personal growth. Here is an interesting worksheet that you can use to assess which type of job really resonates with your passion. I invite you to answer the following questions without any judgment and then study those responses to assess where your interests align with your career choices. Whether you are just getting started with starting a career or you are looking to switch your path, the following exercise will help you self-reflect and assess what can best serve your interest.

Consider the given table and select three things that you value the most:

1. I value _______________________
2. I value _______________________
3. I value _______________________

Table of Values			
Autonomy/ Independence	Education/ Knowledge	Leisure/ Having fun	Personal satisfaction
Beauty	Excellence	Love/ Friendship	Physical comfort
Belonging	Family	Loyalty	Power
Career security	Freedom	Modesty	Prestige/Recognition

Competition	Harmony	Money	Progress/Innovation
Justice	Health	Openness	Promoting Peace
Contributing to society	Honesty/ Sincerity	Optimism	Punctuality
Cooperation	Human Relations	Order	Reaching my full potential
Creativity	Humor	Perseverance	Respect for self and others
Culture/ Language	Integrity	Personal achievement	Social status

Consider the given table and list three of your most defining characteristics:

1. ____________________

2. ____________________

3. ____________________

A Perfectionist	Confident	Down to Earth	Honest	Open	Practical
Adventurous	Convincing	Dynamic	Honorable	Optimistic	Precise
Ambitious	Courageous	Emotional	Imaginative	Organized	Realistic
Analytical	Creative	Enthusiastic	Independent	Original	Reflective
Attentive	Critical	Entrepreneurial	Innovative	Passionate	Reliable
Brave	Curious	Expressive	Innovative	Patient	Reserved/

					Shy
Calm	Demanding	Flexible	Intuitive	Perceptive	Respectful
Careful	Determined	Generous	Likable	Perseverin	Responsible
Cheerful	Disciplined	Helpful	Loyal	Persistent	Serious
Competitive	Discrete	Holistic	Methodical	Positive	Sociable

Consider the given table and list three things you are good at:

1. I am really good at ___________________

2. I am really good at ___________________

3. I am really good at ___________________

Table of Abilities			
Analyzing (text, data)	Making decisions	Using different software	Personal satisfaction
Assembling things	Making lists (of things, priorities)	Using laboratory apparatus	Physical comfort
Classifying objects, documents	Managing stress	Using tools (saw, hammer)	Power
Comparing (things, data)	Manual labor	Working independently	Prestige/Recognition
Composing (text, music)	Navigating online	Working with numbers	Progress/Innovation

Consulting with people	Negotiating	Working with others	Promoting Peace
Creating/Inventing	Operating heavy equipment	Writing (grammar, spelling)	Punctuality
Analyzing (text, data)	Making decisions	Using different software	Personal satisfaction
Developing strategies	Planning Repairing (computers, things)	Using different software	Reaching my full potential
Drawing/Reproduction	Playing a musical instrument	Using laboratory apparatus	Respect for self and others
Driving	Predicting consequences	Using tools (saw, hammer)	Social status
Editing/Correcting text	Preparing text, documents	Working independently	
Establishing systems/processes	Problem-solving		
Explaining or teaching	Public speaking		
Giving good advice	Reading comprehension		
Giving instructions, information	Researching Selling		

Helping others (listening, understanding)	Singing		
Improvising	Summarizing		
Interviewing people	Training animals		

Three Things that you are interested in:

1. I really like _________________________
2. I really like _________________________
3. I really like_________________________

Now list 10 different occupations that you think are the right fit for you as per the abilities, interests and values you have pointed out earlier. Then select the three options that really catch your interest- those will be the career choices that you should seriously consider.

Chapter 2
The Reality of Modern Employment

The reality of modern employment is a complex landscape that is constantly evolving, morphed by technological advancements, shifting market demands, and changing societal norms. Understanding this reality is crucial for each one of us while thriving in the job market today. The rise of the gig economy has transformed the traditional notions of employment. More people are turning towards freelancing, short-term contracts and part-time work. Technology has redefined where and how we work. Remote work options have become more prevalent, breaking geographical barriers. This shift has its advantages, providing work-life balance, but it also blurs the boundaries between professional and personal life. Rapid technological advancements demand continuous upskilling and adaptability. Job roles are evolving, and employers seek individuals who can swiftly learn and adapt to new tools, technologies, and work environments.

There is a growing emphasis on diversity, equity, and inclusion in the workplace. Companies are striving for more diverse teams and inclusive cultures, recognizing the value of varied perspectives and experiences. The modern workplace is increasingly acknowledging the importance of mental health and well-being. Employers are implementing initiatives to support employee mental health, understanding that a healthy workforce is a productive one.

As someone entrenched in the financial landscape, I have witnessed firsthand how these shifts impact the financial stability of every individual. Adaptability has been a cornerstone of modern employment. I have seen clients succeed by embracing continuous learning and evolving with changing job requirements. The importance of diverse and inclusive workplaces is undeniable; they not only foster innovation but also create environments where everyone can thrive. Furthermore, mental health awareness has taken center stage. I have encountered individuals juggling the demands of work while striving to maintain their mental well-being. Employers prioritizing mental health initiatives have seen positive impacts on employee morale and productivity.

The Current Employment Landscape

Ever thought about starting your own thing? You are not alone. More people are ditching the traditional 9-to-5 for freelancing, consulting, and side gigs. The numbers don't lie – about 36% of us are part of this gig economy, doing everything from driving for rideshares to selling handmade crafts on Etsy. In the contemporary job market, the traditional 9-to-5 company job is no longer the sole aspiration. A surge in independent workers, including consultants and freelancers, reflects a growing desire for autonomy, flexibility, and a deeper sense of purpose in one's work. This shift signifies a transformation in the job market, evolving into a dynamic and flexible playground where individuals are not just employees but entrepreneurs in their professional journeys.

For instance, a marketing consultant may choose projects that align with their values, demonstrating the freedom and purpose embedded in independent work. The gig economy witnessed a significant surge in 2008 during the economic downturn, and this trend has continued to intensify. In the face of economic uncertainties, people turned to gig work as a means of financial stability. Fast forward to today, the gig economy has not only sustained its momentum but has grown three times faster than the regular job market. The COVID-19 pandemic further accelerated this growth as individuals sought online platforms for side hustles, emphasizing a fundamental shift in how society perceives and engages in work.

A surprising trend has emerged as more individuals are opting for full-time independent work. Between 2012 and 2021, the number of people pursuing their entrepreneurial endeavors increased by over 50%. This substantial shift in perspective towards work reflects a collective desire for independence, flexibility, and control over professional life. For instance, a graphic designer may choose to freelance full-time, enjoying the freedom to pick projects and clients based on personal preferences.

The current employment landscape is witnessing a significant churn, with individuals increasingly leaving their jobs in pursuit of better pay, flexibility, and more meaningful work. Simultaneously, companies are adapting by prioritizing employee satisfaction, building stronger corporate cultures, and offering remote work options. This reciprocal adaptation reflects a changing dynamic in the employer-employee relationship, emphasizing the need for a mutually beneficial and fulfilling partnership.

Traditional notions of job titles are giving way to a more skill-centric approach to hiring. Companies are getting creative by focusing on skills and abilities rather than rigid job titles. This approach not only helps identify skill gaps within the workforce but also provides opportunities for upskilling and retraining. For instance, a company might hire an individual for their project management skills rather than a predefined job role, fostering a more adaptive and skill-driven workforce.

As the job market remains elusive, companies are redefining their strategies to train and retain their workforce. The employment landscape is evolving rapidly, with certain skills becoming obsolete while new ones emerge. This necessitates a continuous focus on upskilling and adapting to stay relevant in a job scene that is in a constant state of flux. The future of work lies in the hands of those who can navigate this dynamic landscape, continuously enhancing their skill sets to meet the evolving demands of the job market.

The journey from employment to entrepreneurship requires a lot of hard work and commitment for dreamers. This set of journeys involves determination and passion for greater heights. The idea of being a BOSS comes with many responsibilities compared to working for a company whereby income is guaranteed at the end of every working period. In the case of the entrepreneur, those odds take different dimensions altogether, as it comes with critical thinking and perseverance. An entrepreneur has one slogan, which is "Never give up regardless of the obstacle." An entrepreneur always seeks a solution to solve a problem or challenge face be it business or personal, as all both work as one. It is important not to give up in any situation that may come our way, as we all know that challenges may occur but we should use it as an opportunity to grow ourselves. Achieving success requires energy and sacrifice; we should not allow our past to imprison our future; we should use our past as a testament that propels our tomorrow. Many Dreamers foresee themselves as entrepreneurs who are on a journey to great success; they know what it takes and what it involves, so they always prepare for those difficult moments and use the experience to level up their journey. This type of attribute can only be examined through the result of past experience gained during those times of challenges while turning it into a future opportunity.

Importance of Upskilling and Reskilling

"The illiterate of the 21st century will not be those who cannot read and write, but those who cannot learn, unlearn, and relearn." - Alvin Toffler.

In the fast-evolving landscape of work, the importance of upskilling and reskilling cannot be overstated. As technological advancements reshape industries and job requirements, individuals and organizations must embrace continuous learning to stay relevant. Upskilling is all about acquiring new skills or enhancing existing ones to adapt to the changing demands of one's current role or industry. It is about staying ahead of technological advancements, industry trends, and evolving job requirements. For example, an IT professional upskilling might learn a new programming language to excel in their current role or take on additional responsibilities. Reskilling goes a step further by equipping individuals with an entirely new set of skills to transition into a different role or industry. It is a proactive approach to remain employable in the face of job market shifts.

Many dreamers are reluctant to examine their skills and ability to achieve their goals. The idea of self-certification has made the majority of dreamers not strive harder as they become comfortable in their daily endeavors, leaving their bigger picture behind them. It is important to always weigh our skills and set an ambition toward achieving our dreams. Reskills and upskills are paramount in achieving a dream. The ability to seek all the required training, certification, and education that the goals require is very important as this is considered one of the main fuels that guide the success of the dream. It is very pivotal to always seek knowledge whenever a goal is discovered. Having a dream is good, but what are the processes that we put in place to accomplish them? This type of question should be what we evaluate on a daily basis. An example is someone whose ambition is to become a CPA. Such a profession is a great idea, but what are the steps in accomplishing the goal of being a CPA? For someone to become a CPA, he or she must have a minimum Bachelor's degree, have some accounting background, take a CPA board exam, pass the board exam, and have his or her license sponsored by a financial firm. He or she must be willing to work with the sponsoring firm for a couple of months before he can fully practice on his own if she decides. So, a dreamer must not only dream but also put some work behind his ambition. Every individual has an amazing dream, but how many people can put the work into achieving that great dream or idea? The answer is few. We all know that nothing comes easily, as everything is centered on commitment and the ability to step out of our comfort zone. A successful dream accomplishment can only be measured through time management techniques. When we set a dream many times, we forget to include the duration of that great idea and the process in place for it to come to fruition. That is why time management is considered important when setting up a dream. It allows dreamers to track their process, and manage their goals by helping them to break those goals into achievable milestones. Time management serves as a tracker that fuels the milestone journey. Time management plays a crucial role when setting a goal. As a dreamer, time management should be the next process that one can count on in measuring its progress.

Why should time management be this important in achieving a dream? And should this implementation of time management be a thing to be considered? Can one accomplish a dream without managing it properly? What if time management is not a factor in a dream or goal? Does it have any major effect? Why is time management so important to the goal? All these questions allow someone to evaluate how big is the dream planned to achieve, including its importance. There are some dreams that contain inventions, ideas, and discoveries that are centered on public benefit/interest. This type of dream is considered huge and requires intensive and proper time management delegation, including third processes. If we look at those great inventions and how they were able to accomplish them, we will now understand the importance of time management. There is no small dream/goal. Once a dream is always a dream. An idea remains an idea, whether big or small, as long it addresses problems and presents solutions to self and public needs. That is why dreams require human sacrifices such as time management, delegation, discipline, coordination, skills, knowledge, and self-belief. As a dreamer, one must always be the first person to believe in his dream. Once he or she is very confident that his dream is legitimate, it gives others the opportunity to listen to his ideas. The act of self-confidence in a dream with the acting process of making sure those great ideas come to fruition can only be examined by the doers. There are many dreamers, but fewer are actually considered the action-takers, which are the doers.

Economic Growth and Innovation:

Nations and industries benefit from a workforce skilled in the latest technologies and methodologies. Upskilling and reskilling initiatives contribute to economic growth by fostering innovation and ensuring that industries remain at the forefront of advancements. The World Economic Forum warns that by 2025, 50% of all employees will need reskilling. PwC's report complements this concern, revealing that a significant 74% of CEOs worry about the availability of key skills in their workforce.

Job Satisfaction and Personal Growth:

Beyond professional considerations, upskilling and reskilling contribute to job satisfaction and personal growth. Individuals find fulfillment in expanding their skill sets, taking on new challenges, and achieving milestones in their careers. According to the World Economic Forum, by 2025, the time spent on current tasks at work by humans and machines will be equal. The McKinsey Global Institute estimates that around 375 million workers (14% of the global workforce) may need to switch occupational categories by 2030 due to automation. As technology continues to advance, jobs are transforming. The ability to learn and adapt is becoming a core skill. Alvin Toffler's quote encapsulates the essence of the future – it is not just about what you know now but your capacity to learn anew.

Closing the Skills Gap: Nurturing Passion for Continuous Improvement

The modern age often witnesses a mismatch between the skills individuals possess and those demanded by industries. Upskilling and reskilling play a crucial role in mitigating these skills gaps, creating a more harmonious alignment between the workforce and industry needs. Steve Jobs, the visionary co-founder of Apple, left us with a profound insight: "The only way to do great work is to love what you do." This sentiment resonates deeply with the pressing need to close the skills gap in the workforce. According to a World Economic Forum study, by 2025, the skills gap is projected to leave 12 million workers without the necessary skills. Deloitte's survey adds weight to this concern, revealing that a staggering 94% of executives consider closing the skills gap a critical business challenge. It is not merely about plugging holes in skill sets; it is about cultivating a genuine love for continuous improvement. Organizations recognize the urgency in addressing this skills gap, understanding that a passionate and skilled workforce is integral to sustainable business success. Jobs' philosophy encourages a shift in mindset, viewing the process of acquiring new skills as an opportunity for personal and professional fulfillment.

Jeffrey Nelson Cole

"The key to pursuing excellence is to embrace an organic, long-term learning process and not to live in a shell of static, safe mediocrity."

Josh Waitzkin

This philosophy resonates strongly with the imperative of fostering innovation and agility through upskilling. A study by Capgemini reveals that 61% of organizations consider upskilling crucial for achieving innovation objectives. The Boston Consulting Group further supports this by noting that companies with a strong learning culture exhibit 37% greater employee productivity. Continuous learning is not just about acquiring new skills; it is about adapting to change, embracing challenges, and breaking away from the comfort of mediocrity. Upskilling and reskilling initiatives, as illustrated by these statistics, contribute not only to individual relevance but also to the organizational dynamism required for innovation and agility in a rapidly evolving landscape.

Pursuing Your Quintessential Dream Job

Whether you are at the outset of your career or contemplating a significant shift, the pursuit of your dream job involves intentional steps, self-reflection, and a commitment to realizing your professional aspirations. At the heart of pursuing your quintessential dream job lies a deep understanding of your passion and purpose. Reflect on what truly excites you, the activities that make time fly, and the causes that ignite your enthusiasm. Your dream job should align with your values, allowing you to derive fulfillment and satisfaction beyond monetary rewards. Conduct thorough research on the industry, the skills required, and the key players. Leverage informational interviews, networking events, and online resources to gain insights into the day-to-day realities of the role. Use this information not only to refine your aspirations but also to tailor your skills and experiences accordingly.

Dream jobs often demand a specific set of skills and qualifications. Identify the competencies required for your desired role and invest in acquiring or honing them. This might involve pursuing additional education certifications or gaining practical experience through internships or freelance projects. Continuously seek opportunities to enhance your skill set and stay abreast of industry trends.

As you venture into pursuing your dream job, curate a compelling narrative that communicates your unique value proposition. Your resume, cover letter, and online presence should vividly articulate how your skills, experiences, and values align with the requirements of your dream role. Showcase not just what you have done but how it contributes to the narrative of why you are the ideal candidate.

Attend industry events, engage in online forums, and seek mentorship from professionals who have trodden a similar path. Networking not only provides valuable insights but also opens doors to potential opportunities and collaborations. The pursuit of a dream job is seldom a linear journey. Anticipate challenges, setbacks, and moments of uncertainty. Cultivate resilience and perseverance as your companions on this odyssey. Learn from setbacks, adapt your strategy, and stay committed to the vision of landing your quintessential role.

Once you have positioned yourself as a strong candidate, navigate the hiring process with finesse. Hone your interview skills, craft compelling responses to common questions, and showcase your enthusiasm for the role. Be prepared for assessments, case studies, or presentations that demonstrate your practical aptitude for the position.

As you approach the culmination of your pursuit, navigate the negotiation phase thoughtfully. Understand your worth in the context of the role and industry standards. Negotiate not just for financial compensation but also for benefits, work-life balance, and any other factors that contribute to your overall job satisfaction.

The Journey from Employment to Entrepreneurship

The journey from employment to entrepreneurship is a transformative odyssey that requires a mix of vision, courage, and strategic planning. This metamorphosis often begins with a realization—a spark of inspiration or a deep-seated desire for autonomy and purpose beyond the confines of a traditional job. For many, the journey starts with a feeling of dissatisfaction or an unshakeable sense that there is more to achieve and contribute than the routine of a 9-to-5 job allows. It is a recognition that personal aspirations and untapped potential could be harnessed in a way that traditional employment might not fully allow. This realization acts as the catalyst for exploring the uncharted territory of entrepreneurship.

The foundation of this journey rests on a clear vision. Entrepreneurs need to identify a problem they are passionate about solving or a market gap that intrigues them. Concurrently, possessing or acquiring the necessary skills to navigate the entrepreneurial landscape is essential. Adaptability, resilience, and a willingness to learn are crucial attributes. Risk tolerance is another vital requirement. The shift from a stable job to entrepreneurship often involves financial uncertainty, requiring a mindset ready to embrace challenges and weather uncertainties.

Here, I cannot help but share the inspiring journey of Lucas, a former student of mine. He is a software engineer who spent years working for a prominent tech corporation. While the job provided financial stability, Lucas harbored a burning passion for creating innovative solutions to common problems. Fueled by a vision of simplifying complex processes through technology, he decided to transition from employment to entrepreneurship.

Lucas' journey began with evenings spent sketching out ideas on a notepad and attending industry conferences to stay updated on the latest trends. Recognizing a gap in the market for a user-friendly project management tool, Lucas started developing a prototype during weekends and after work hours. The journey was not without challenges. He faced skepticism from peers, encountered technical hurdles, and grappled with the fear of leaving a stable job. However, fueled by the hope of bringing a unique solution to the market, he persisted.

With a meticulously crafted business plan and a prototype in hand, Lucas took the leap. The hustle intensified as networking efforts led to seed investment, enabling the formal launch of the project management tool. As word spread about its efficiency, businesses embraced Lucas' creation.

What started as a dream transformed into a successful tech startup. Lucas' story exemplifies the journey from employment to entrepreneurship—driven by a vision, supported by skills, fueled by hope, and sustained by relentless hustle.

Chapter 3
Traditional Careers vs Entrepreneurship

In the vast landscape of career choices, people often find themselves standing at a crucial crossroads, faced with two prominent paths: entrepreneurship and traditional careers. Both avenues present a diverse array of experiences, challenges, and rewards, and the choice between them becomes a pivotal decision in shaping one's professional journey. The question looms: Which path is the right fit for you? The decision between entrepreneurship and a traditional career is not a one-size-fits-all choice. It is a deeply personal odyssey influenced by factors like risk tolerance, passion, and the desire for autonomy. Entrepreneurs thrive on the excitement of the unknown, relishing the freedom to shape their destiny. Traditional career enthusiasts find fulfillment in the stability, structure, and defined growth trajectories provided by established organizations.

Understanding Traditional Careers

Traditional careers are similar to seasoned classics in the world of work. They are the jobs that follow the well-trodden paths within established organizations or industries. Think of them as the reliable, go-to choices that have been around for a while. These careers come with a set structure, clear roles, and a step-by-step approach to climbing the professional ladder. So, in a traditional career, you typically start off by getting the education needed for your chosen field. Once you are in the workforce, you navigate through different levels in a kind of corporate hierarchy. This is not a free-for-all; there is a system in place and you move up the ranks through promotions and hitting certain milestones. It is like following a map where each step is laid out for you.

What Makes Traditional Careers Tick?

- **Hierarchy in Action:** Picture an organization like a pyramid with different levels of authority. Traditional careers work within this structured hierarchy, where everyone has their place.

- **Job Descriptions to the Rescue**: Your role in a traditional career is pretty clearly defined. You know what you are supposed to do, and tasks are assigned based on your position in the hierarchy.

- **Step-by-Step Advancement**: Career progression in traditional paths is like climbing stairs – one step at a time. You start at the bottom, gain experience, perform well, and move up the ladder.

- **Specializing in Something:** Traditional careers often mean becoming an expert in a specific industry or field. You pick a lane and become really good at what you do, contributing to the overall success of the organization.

- **Steady Ground and Job Security**: A big perk of traditional careers is stability. You get regular paychecks, benefits, and a certain level of predictability in your professional life. It is like having a solid foundation under your feet.

While traditional careers are still very much a thing, it is worth noting that the job scene is changing. There are newer models like remote work, gig economies, and entrepreneurship that are shaking things up. So, while traditional careers provide a solid and reliable option, there is a whole world of different paths out there to explore. It is like having a variety of flavors to choose from in the career buffet! Traditional careers, once considered the epitome of stability, are encountering a shifting landscape marked by a series of challenges. As the professional world evolves, those who are exploring traditional paths find themselves grappling with the following:

- ***Rapid Technological Advancements:*** Traditional careers often face the challenge of keeping pace with rapid technological changes. As industries undergo digital transformations, individuals in traditional roles may find themselves at a disadvantage if they don't adapt and acquire new digital skills.

- ***Job Redundancy and Automation***: Automation and artificial intelligence are reshaping industries, leading to the redundancy of certain traditional roles. Jobs that were once deemed secure may now be at risk, necessitating upskilling or transitioning to roles that are less susceptible to automation.

- ***Limited Flexibility and Work-Life Balance:*** Many traditional careers come with a rigid structure, limiting flexibility and work-life balance. The changing expectations of the workforce, especially with the rise of remote work and flexible schedules, pose a challenge to traditional work models that favor a more conventional approach.

- ***Hierarchy and Bureaucracy:*** Traditional organizations often maintain hierarchical structures and bureaucratic processes.

Going through layers of hierarchy can impede innovation and slow down decision-making processes, hindering the agility required in today's dynamic business environment.

- ***Generational Shifts in Work Values***: With the entry of younger generations into the workforce, there is a noticeable shift in work values. Millennials and Generation Z prioritize factors such as purpose, meaningful work, and a healthy work-life balance, challenging the traditional emphasis solely on job security and stability.

The World of Entrepreneurship

"The best way to predict the future is to create it."

- Peter Drucker

Peter Drucker's words echo the spirit of entrepreneurship, a realm where we are not merely spectators of the future but active creators of our destinies. The world is undergoing a significant shift toward entrepreneurship, transforming the way we perceive and engage with work. The advent of the digital age has been a game-changer for aspiring entrepreneurs. The democratization of access to information and resources has significantly lowered the barriers to entry. Entrepreneurs can leverage technology to research, plan, and launch ventures more efficiently. Moreover, technological advancements have become a catalyst for innovation, allowing entrepreneurs to disrupt traditional industries and create entirely new ones. For instance, the rise of e-commerce, artificial intelligence, and blockchain technology has opened up unprecedented opportunities for those with an entrepreneurial spirit.

Modern professionals, particularly younger generations, are reshaping the traditional notions of work. Autonomy, purpose, and flexibility have become paramount values. Entrepreneurship aligns seamlessly with these preferences, offering individuals the chance to create businesses that reflect their passions and values. The desire for meaningful work and a sense of ownership drives many to venture into entrepreneurship, where they can shape their careers in alignment with their personal and professional aspirations.

The interconnectedness of the world through the internet has transformed the business landscape. Entrepreneurs are no longer confined to local markets; they can tap into a global audience. This global connectivity opens up new markets, diverse consumer bases, and unprecedented growth opportunities for startups. Small businesses can leverage digital platforms to reach customers worldwide, facilitating the growth of startups and encouraging the development of a robust global entrepreneurial ecosystem. Whether it is through e-commerce platforms, remote work, or international collaborations, entrepreneurs now have the tools to expand their reach far beyond geographical boundaries.

"The entrepreneur always searches for change, responds to it, and exploits it as an opportunity."

Peter Drucker

Entrepreneurship is more than just starting a business; it is a dynamic process that involves identifying opportunities, marshaling resources, and exploring uncertainties to create value. It encompasses various forms, from small startups disrupting industries to corporate entrepreneurship within established organizations.

Take the example of Airbnb. It was founded by Brian Chesky, and it changed the whole hospitality industry by connecting travelers with unique accommodations. The platform leveraged technology to create a decentralized lodging marketplace, challenging traditional hotel models and providing new income opportunities for hosts. Airbnb revolutionized the concept of hospitality by transforming spare rooms and unique properties into desirable accommodations. The platform enabled hosts to open their homes to travelers, offering a personalized and often more affordable alternative to traditional hotels. By embracing the sharing economy, Airbnb tapped into a global network of hosts and guests, fostering a sense of community and cultural exchange.

The success of Airbnb is deeply rooted in its use of technology to decentralize the lodging market. The platform's user-friendly interface, secure payment systems, and review features facilitated trust between hosts and guests. By leveraging technology, Airbnb made it possible for individuals to participate in the hospitality industry without the need for a traditional hotel infrastructure. One of Airbnb's significant impacts is the economic empowerment it provides to hosts. Ordinary individuals could now monetize their extra space, creating supplementary income streams. This shift in the economic landscape empowered hosts, democratizing the hospitality sector and challenging the conventional hierarchy of the industry.

Why is entrepreneurship on the Rise?

Entrepreneurs have the freedom to shape their ventures according to their vision. This autonomy fosters creativity and allows for innovative solutions to emerge. Unlike traditional employment, where decisions may be top-down, entrepreneurs can experiment, pivot, and implement their ideas. Entrepreneurs can address societal challenges through their ventures. By identifying and solving problems, they contribute to positive social and economic change. The ability to create meaningful impact adds a sense of purpose to entrepreneurial endeavors. Successful entrepreneurship can lead to substantial financial rewards. Entrepreneurs have the opportunity to build wealth through the growth and success of their ventures. While financial success is not guaranteed, the potential for significant rewards serves as a motivational factor.

While the benefits are enticing, entrepreneurship also comes with its share of ***challenges***:

There is an inherent uncertainty and risk-taking factor in entrepreneurship. The future is unpredictable, and entrepreneurs must navigate challenges without guaranteed outcomes. This risk can be a barrier for those who seek stability and predictability. Starting a venture often requires significant resources, and entrepreneurs may face challenges in securing funding, talent, or other critical resources. Limited resources can impede the execution of business plans and growth strategies.

The dedication required to build a successful venture can impact work-life balance. Entrepreneurs often find themselves fully immersed in their work, which can lead to challenges in their personal lives. Balancing the demands of entrepreneurship with personal well-being requires intentional effort.

Entrepreneurial ventures operate in competitive markets. Staying ahead requires constant innovation and adaptability to outpace competitors. Exploring market dynamics and standing out in a crowded landscape is a perpetual challenge for entrepreneurs. While entrepreneurship offers autonomy, impact, and financial rewards, it also comes with challenges that demand resilience, resourcefulness, and a willingness to embrace uncertainty. As the world continues to shift toward entrepreneurship, individuals are empowered to be not just spectators but active contributors to the evolving narrative of innovation and progress.

The Shift from Employment to Business

In recent years, there has been a noticeable global shift from the traditional model of employment to a surge in entrepreneurial endeavors. This evolution is driven by various factors, including changing attitudes toward work, technological advancements, and a desire for greater autonomy. Let's explore this paradigm shift with real-life examples and research studies that illuminate the trends shaping the transition from employment to business ownership.

1. Rise of the Gig Economy:

The gig economy has witnessed a significant surge with platforms like Uber, Airbnb, and Upwork, reshaping how people approach work. This trend allows individuals to tap into their skills or assets to earn income without adhering to traditional employment structures. A McKinsey Global Institute report indicates that as much as 20-30% of the working-age population in Europe and the United States, totaling up to 162 million people, engage in independent work. This shift has provided workers with flexibility and autonomy, challenging conventional notions of employment.

2. Technological Empowerment:

Technological advancements, particularly in e-commerce platforms like Shopify and Amazon, have empowered individuals to become entrepreneurs by starting their online businesses. This has not only facilitated a global reach but also expanded the customer base for small ventures. According to an Intuit study, the rise of freelancers, contractors, and temporary workers is projected to constitute 40% of the American workforce by 2020, with technology platforms playing a crucial role in enabling this shift toward independent work.

3. Changing Work Culture:

Leading companies such as Google and Atlassian have actively fostered entrepreneurial cultures within their organizations. They encourage employees to explore and develop innovative ideas, blurring the lines between traditional job roles. Deloitte's Millennial Survey underscores this shift, revealing that 76% of millennials view business ownership as a viable career choice. This reflects a broader transformation in attitudes toward embracing entrepreneurial endeavors, even within the framework of established corporate structures.

4. Remote Work and Digital Nomadism:

The rise of digital nomads symbolizes a broader shift towards flexible work arrangements and location-independent businesses. Remote work has become a norm, and studies, such as the one by Buffer and AngelList, indicate that 98% of remote workers wish to continue working remotely. This signals a growing preference for non-traditional work setups, driven by advancements in technology that facilitate seamless communication and collaboration irrespective of geographical constraints.

5. Entrepreneurial Education and Support:

Initiatives like startup incubators, accelerators, and educational programs, exemplified by institutions like Y Combinator and Techstars, play a crucial role in nurturing aspiring entrepreneurs. This support ecosystem helps facilitate the launch of new businesses by providing mentorship, resources, and a conducive environment for innovation. The Global Entrepreneurship Monitor (GEM) reports a rising trend in entrepreneurial education, with over 77% of the world's economies offering courses dedicated to fostering entrepreneurial skills.

6. Financial Technology (Fintech) and Crowdfunding:

Financial technology (Fintech) has transformed the landscape of funding for entrepreneurial ventures. Platforms like Kickstarter and Indiegogo have democratized access to capital by allowing entrepreneurs to fund their projects through crowdfunding. This has opened up new avenues for securing financial support beyond traditional banking systems. A World Bank report underscores the transformative impact of fintech on financial inclusion, providing entrepreneurs with alternative financing options and reducing barriers to entry in the business landscape.

Finding the Right Fit for You

In a world teeming with diverse career options, the quest for the right fit calls for introspection, research, and a keen understanding of personal values and aspirations. We all are unique, with different sets of strengths and weaknesses. The opportunities are open for everyone; we just have to assess which one can best meet our life expectations and values. I never tell my clients to ditch their traditional careers for entrepreneurship, nor do I push anyone to pursue a 9-5 job; all I recommend to people is to follow their instincts, interests, and values and then see where they take them. The following table draws a comparison between entrepreneurship and traditional careers based on the type of personality characteristics required to pursue them. Let's go through them and then assess which one is right for you:

Personality Characteristic	Entrepreneurship	Traditional Careers
Risk-Taking	High tolerance for risk, comfortable with uncertainty.	Lower risk tolerance prefers stability and predictability.
Innovativeness	Creative, enjoys thinking outside the box, and seeks new ideas.	Adheres to established processes and values stability.

Adaptability	Quick to adapt to change, thrive in dynamic environments.	Prefers structured routines and may be resistant to frequent changes.
Independence	Self-reliant, enjoys autonomy and makes independent decisions.	Values collaboration and may thrive in a team-oriented environment.
Persistence	Resilient and persistent in overcoming challenges and setbacks.	Adaptable and persistent, but may prefer a stable environment.
Visionary Thinking	Forward-thinking, ability to see long-term goals and strategies.	Focuses on immediate goals and may not prioritize long-term vision.
Leadership	Natural leadership qualities, comfortable leading others.	May excel in roles with defined leadership hierarchies.
Flexibility	Flexible in approaches and strategies, open to experimentation.	May prefer structured processes and may find comfort in routine.
Stress Management	Handles stress well and sees challenges as opportunities.	May seek stability and avoid situations causing high-stress levels.
Decision-Making Style	Quick decision-maker, comfortable with making bold choices.	May prefer a more deliberative decision-making process.
Team Orientation	Can work independently but also collaborates effectively in teams.	Prefers working within established team structures.

So, to sum it up, choosing between entrepreneurship and a traditional career is a big decision, but it doesn't have to be overwhelming. There is a simple six steps formula that you can put to use:

First, Know Yourself: Start by digging deep into what truly makes you tick. What activities make you lose track of time? What topics could you talk about for hours on end? Understanding your passions and the skills that bring you joy is like turning on the headlights for your journey – it illuminates the path ahead.

Prioritize Your Must-Haves: Next up, think about your life priorities. Is having a balanced work-life equation a top priority, or are you excited by the idea of diving into the hustle? Consider your financial needs – are you comfortable with a bit of unpredictability, or is a stable income your comfort zone? Knowing these must-haves is like creating a checklist for your journey – it helps filter out the noise.

Explore Your Options: Imagine this as trying on different outfits before a big event. Delve into the day-to-day realities of both entrepreneurship and traditional careers. What kind of skills are in demand? How can you expect to grow? It's like strolling through a shopping mall, exploring and trying on different possibilities for your future.

Check Out Other Travelers: Connect with those who have already explored these journeys. Chat with entrepreneurs and 9-to-5ers alike. Their stories and advice are like postcards from different destinations – full of insights and wisdom. Networking and mentorship act as your travel guides, giving you a glimpse into the road ahead.

Test the Waters: Consider this as sampling a dish before committing to the whole meal. Engage in internships, part-time roles, or side hustles to get a taste of the work environment. It's like taking a test drive to see if the work vibe aligns with your preferences.

Embrace the Journey: And finally, remember that your career path is a dynamic journey, not a one-time decision. Just like a road trip, be open to changing routes, exploring new places, and adapting to the changing landscape. The journey is as important as the destination – embrace every twist and turn with curiosity and resilience.

As a financial specialist, my journey began with introspection – I wasn't just absorbing knowledge; I was breaking barriers. I found myself immersed in discussions about market trends, investment strategies, and economic analysis for hours on end. That clarity illuminated my path forward.

I craved a dynamic career but also valued a semblance of work-life balance. Stability in income was crucial, yet I was willing to navigate some unpredictability for growth opportunities. It was like creating a roadmap, filtering out distractions that didn't align with my goals. I knew this world often favored a select few, and I was determined to stand out. My days were packed with classes, followed by a part-time job at night, all while relentlessly pursuing a vision that only I could see so clearly. For me, finance wasn't solely about profits; it was about empowering others and creating opportunities where none seemed to exist before. My journey wasn't just about mastering the field; it was about transforming lives through the artistry of financial expertise. Each experience and each challenge has added depth and meaning to my path. And that's what I recommend to everyone! Go out there and explore! The more you discover, the more you learn about yourself and the world around you.

Chapter 4
The Power of Perseverance:

"Success is not the end; failure is not the end either. It is having the guts to keep going that really matters."

Winston Churchill

Think of your life as this crazy adventure full of ups and downs. The thing that helps you keep going when things get wild is called perseverance. It acts as your own personal guide through all the craziness. And guess what? If you are dreaming big, especially about being a boss or reaching the tippy top of the success ladder, perseverance is like your superpower. It turns tough times into lessons and dreams into real things. So, as you flip through the pages of life, check out the stories of people who made it big. You will see how their never-give-up attitude led them to awesome places.

You see, life has not always been a smooth ride for me, but the one thing that's been my constant companion is perseverance. Growing up on the lively West African coast in Liberia, I learned early on that challenges are just part of the journey. When I was 20, I decided to embrace uncertainties and that habit has taken me through a rollercoaster of experiences. I firmly believe that leadership is about service and elevating others. It is a philosophy that has guided me in my career and in life. Through my experiences, I have come to see that perseverance is not just about pushing through tough times – it is about turning those tough times into opportunities.

Inspiring Stories of Perseverance

When we look into the life stories of the most successful people and entrepreneurs today, a common thread binds their narratives to perseverance. It becomes evident that their triumphs are not merely a result of innate talent or luck but rather a testament to their unwavering commitment to persevere. Regardless of the industry, background, or challenges faced, these individuals share a relentless determination to keep going, undeterred by failures or obstacles. Resilience becomes their guiding force, fueling a journey marked by setbacks, rejections, and adversities. It is the tenacity to stand up after each fall, the refusal to succumb to discouragement, that sets them apart. In the face of uncertainty, they chose to press on, and in doing so, they shaped their destinies. The stories of today's most successful figures echo the resounding truth that success is often a product of perseverance-a quality that transforms dreams into reality and adversity into stepping stones toward greatness.

Soichiro Honda

Have you heard about the incredible life journey of Soichiro Honda, the visionary founder of Honda? His story is a powerful testament to the unwavering strength of perseverance. In the early 1940s, Honda faced rejection from Toyota, a setback that could have easily crushed his entrepreneurial spirit. Undeterred, he harnessed this setback as fuel for his determination to succeed. In 1948, amidst the post-war economic challenges in Japan, Honda established the Honda Motor Company, starting with the production of motorized bicycles. The path to success, however, was fraught with financial struggles. In 1953, the company faced near collapse due to the failure of its first complete motorcycle, the Dream. Despite this setback, Honda's perseverance shone through. He re-evaluated, learned from the experience, and went on to develop the successful Super Cub in 1958, a model that became the world's best-selling motor vehicle.

Through the 1960s and 1970s, Honda expanded its global footprint. The introduction of the Civic in 1972 and the Accord in 1976 marked Honda's entry into the American automobile market. By the early 1980s, Honda had become a leading force in the automotive industry, setting records for fuel efficiency and reliability. Soichiro Honda's journey is a story of resilience in the face of adversity, a saga of turning rejection and financial setbacks into groundbreaking success. Today, Honda stands as a global automotive giant with a legacy built on the indomitable spirit of its founder. Soichiro Honda's story exemplifies how steadfast perseverance, coupled with a relentless pursuit of excellence, can elevate an individual from rejection and hardship to the pinnacle of success.

J. K. Rowling

Have you caught wind of J.K. Rowling's incredible journey? Her life story is a true testament to the power of perseverance. If you have not heard about it, get ready for an inspiring ride. Rowling faced some serious struggles before becoming the mega-successful author we know today. In the early '90s, she was a single mom, living on welfare, and her "Harry Potter" manuscript faced rejection from multiple publishers. Despite these setbacks, Rowling did not throw in the towel. In 1997, the first book, "Harry Potter and the Philosopher's Stone" (or "Sorcerer's Stone" in the U.S.), hit the shelves and the wizarding world took off.

Rowling's perseverance continued to shine. By 1999, she became the first author to earn more than a billion dollars from book sales. However, her journey was not all smooth. In the early 2000s, she faced personal challenges, including the loss of her mother and a divorce. Yet, Rowling pressed on. She expanded the magical universe with more books, and the film adaptations became blockbusters.

By 2011, Forbes named her the first author to become a billionaire and she is consistently listed among the world's wealthiest women. Rowling's story is a rollercoaster of triumphs over hardships, a true embodiment of perseverance. It is proof that even when life throws its toughest spells, standing tall and forging ahead can lead to extraordinary success. J.K. Rowling's journey encourages us all to believe in our magic, no matter how tough the journey may seem.

Spanx Founder

Sara Blakely, the founder of Spanx, whose entrepreneurial journey is a testament to perseverance and ingenuity. In the late 1990s, Sara Blakely was selling fax machines door-to-door and dreaming of a more comfortable undergarment solution. Fueled by a passion for innovation, she took $5,000 in savings and started working on her idea for a footless pantyhose. Blakely faced numerous rejections from hosiery mills before finally finding one willing to produce the revolutionary product.

In 2000, armed with a patent for her invention, Blakely launched Spanx from her apartment. She faced initial challenges, from convincing department stores to stock her product to competing with established lingerie brands. However, her perseverance paid off. Oprah Winfrey endorsed Spanx on her show, and the brand gained widespread popularity.

Blakely's journey was not without hurdles. In 2012, she faced setbacks when Spanx had to recall a line of leggings due to quality issues. Instead of being defeated, Blakely saw it as an opportunity to learn and improve. Spanx continued to grow, expanding its product line beyond shapewear to include leggings, bras, and activewear. In 2012, Sara Blakely became the world's youngest self-made female billionaire. Her story showcases how resilience, coupled with a unique idea and unwavering determination, can transform a simple concept into a globally recognized and successful brand. Sara Blakely's entrepreneurial spirit and ability to turn challenges into opportunities inspire aspiring business leaders around the world.

Jack Ma

Jack Ma, the co-founder of Alibaba Group, whose journey from humble beginnings to becoming a global business icon is a compelling tale of perseverance and entrepreneurial spirit.

Jack Ma, born in Hangzhou, China, faced numerous setbacks early in his life. He failed his college entrance exams twice but was determined to overcome adversity. After completing his studies, he faced rejection from multiple jobs, including KFC, where 24 applicants were hired, and he was the only one rejected. Undeterred, Ma continued to persevere. In 1999, during a trip to the United States, Ma discovered the internet and realized its vast potential. Inspired, he founded Alibaba from his apartment in Hangzhou with the vision of connecting Chinese manufacturers with global buyers. The early days of Alibaba were challenging, with the company facing skepticism and the difficulties of exploring the rapidly evolving tech landscape.

Jack Ma's perseverance and strategic vision led Alibaba to overcome these challenges. The company grew into an e-commerce giant, transforming the way businesses operate in China and globally. Alibaba's initial public offering (IPO) on the New York Stock Exchange in 2014 was one of the largest in history, further solidifying Ma's position as a leading entrepreneur. Despite his remarkable success, Jack Ma continued to face hurdles. In 2018, he stepped down as Alibaba's executive chairman, marking a transition in leadership. This move, however, reflected Ma's forward-thinking approach, emphasizing the importance of succession planning and adapting to change.

Jack Ma's journey teaches us valuable lessons about resilience and embracing challenges. His ability to turn rejection into motivation, navigate uncertainties, and envision the potential of the internet has made him an influential figure in the business world. Jack Ma's story is a testament to the transformative power of perseverance, innovation, and a never-give-up attitude.

The Impact of Resilience on Success

As the saying goes, "It is not whether you get knocked down; it is whether you get up." This timeless quote by Vince Lombardi encapsulates the essence of resilience and perseverance in the pursuit of success. In a world often fixated on overnight achievements, it is crucial to recognize that lasting success is not a product of quick wins but rather a result of years of relentless perseverance and unwavering efforts. Success that comes too easily tends to be fleeting, lacking the robust foundation that can weather storms and challenges. The effects of resilience on success are profound and multifaceted, shaping the trajectory of individuals and organizations in their pursuit of goals. With resilience as your sidekick:

You Bounce Back from Tough Times:

Resilience helps people deal with tough situations and come out stronger. Instead of giving up when things go wrong, resilient people see problems as chances to learn and get better. It is similar to turning a stumble into a step forward. Think about Walt Disney. Before Disney became a big deal, he faced money troubles and got rejected. But he did not give up. His resilience turned his problems into a path to creating Disney magic.

You Roll with Changes:

Resilient people can handle changes well. They do not get stuck in one way of doing things; they are good at adjusting when things around them change. This skill is super important in a world that's always evolving. Look at Steve Jobs from Apple. He faced problems and even got kicked out of his own company. But he did not quit. He came back and made Apple a huge success with cool products like the iPhone.

You Feel Sure of Yourself:

Resilience makes you feel sure you can handle challenges. When you succeed because you bounced back from tough times, it gives you confidence. You start thinking, "I can do this!" and that makes it easier to tackle new challenges. Take Oprah Winfrey. From a tough start, she became a big deal in the media world. Her resilience showed in her confidence to try new things and succeed in different projects.

You Do Not Give Up Easily:

Resilience means sticking with your goals even when things get hard. It is the ability to keep going, even if you fail a few times. This determination is what helps you stay focused on what you want to achieve. Think about Thomas Edison, the guy who invented the light bulb. He failed a lot before he got it right. But he did not stop trying, and his resilience lit up the world.

You Thinking Outside the Box:

Resilience makes you creative and open to new ideas. When you can bounce back from tough situations, you are more likely to come up with cool and different ways of doing things. Look at Elon Musk, the guy behind SpaceX and Tesla. His resilience lets him think of new solutions for big problems, changing how we do things in space and with electric cars.

A few years back, I crossed paths with a client named Henry, who walked into my office with a dream and determination to dive into the real estate world. Now, Henry was a go-getter, but he faced the classic hurdles – not much experience and a wallet that echoed emptiness when it came to starting a business. As a financial consultant, my job was to turn that dream into a tangible plan. After some thorough brainstorming and a couple of late-night sessions, we hatched a strategy. Henry decided to take a leap of faith and invest in properties in areas experiencing a dip in prices. It was a bold move, especially considering the risks involved, but he was adamant about making his mark in real estate.

Over the years, Henry's journey resembled a roller coaster. Countless deals brought both triumphs and challenges, but his resilience and determination never wavered. The market threw curveballs, and unexpected setbacks arose, yet Henry stood his ground. There were moments when it felt like the dream was slipping away, but every obstacle became a stepping stone. Henry's journey was a testament to the transformative power of resilience. He weathered storms in the real estate market, faced financial uncertainties, and navigated the intricacies of deals gone awry. Each setback was a lesson, each challenge a chance to grow.

Fast forward to today, and Henry is not just a real estate entrepreneur; he runs his own successful company. The years of persistence, learning from mistakes, and an unwavering belief in his vision have made him an experienced and established figure in the real estate industry. In Henry's story, I witnessed firsthand how resilience, coupled with strategic planning and a dash of courage, can turn a novice dreamer into a seasoned entrepreneur. It is not just about the properties he bought or sold; it is about the grit and determination that shaped his journey. As a consultant, it is stories like Henry's that make this profession not just about numbers and strategies but about transforming dreams into tangible success.

When Persistence Meets Opportunity

"Opportunity does not knock; it presents itself when you beat down the door."

When persistence meets opportunity, a powerful synergy unfolds, creating a fertile ground for success and achievement. Persistence is the unwavering commitment to achieving a goal despite challenges, setbacks, or obstacles. On the other hand, opportunity represents a favorable set of circumstances that can be seized for advancement or progress. When these two forces intersect:

You Seize the Moment: You know that feeling when something awesome comes your way, and you grab it with both hands? Well, persistence is like your superhero power in those moments. It helps you not just see opportunities but jump on them. Challenges do not scare you; they are more like chances to get closer to your dreams. So, when the perfect opportunity shows up, you are all set to make the most of it.

You Turn Setbacks into Set-Ups: Think of setbacks as those potholes on the road to success. Now, persistent people do not let those bumps stop them; they see them as lessons. So, when a new opportunity comes around, you are not just ready; you are using all those lessons to navigate it like a pro, turning setbacks into stepping stones.

You Build Expertise: Imagine expertise as your secret weapon. Persistent people become masters in what they love doing. And guess what? This expertise helps you spot opportunities others might miss. So, when a cool chance comes knocking, you are not just opening the door; you are doing a victory dance because you are totally prepared.

You Create a Ripple Effect: Now, think of persistence and opportunity as a tag team. When you are persistently chasing your goals, it is the same as throwing a pebble into a calm pond. The ripples? Those are the good things that start coming your way. Success attracts more success, and suddenly, you are at the center of a pool of awesome opportunities.

You Achieve Breakthroughs: Ever had those moments when everything just clicked? That's what happens when persistence and opportunity join forces. These breakthroughs are when all your hard work pays off, and you achieve something huge that once seemed impossible.

You Build a Legacy: Lastly, think of building a legacy as creating your own storybook. Every challenge you overcome, every opportunity you seize, becomes a part of your narrative. Your story is not just about hitting goals; it is about leaving a mark that inspires others.

Back in the 1950s, Ray Kroc was just an ordinary guy with a fierce determination to make it on his own. He had no big savings, no groundbreaking idea of his own. But he was persistent as heck. One day, he stumbled upon a little local fast-food joint called McDonald's, run by the McDonald brothers. Ray was blown away by their system and the potential he saw. He did not just see burgers and fries; he saw an opportunity for something massive. Now, here is the kicker: Ray was in his 50s at that time. Most people would think, "Hey, maybe it is time to take it easy," but not Ray.

In 1954, he convinced the McDonald brothers to let him franchise their brand. This was the start of something huge, but it was not all smooth sailing. Ray faced rejection after rejection when trying to get investors. But did he give up? Nope. His famous quote says it all, "I was an overnight success alright, but 30 years is a long, long night." Ray Kroc's journey was like a rollercoaster. He opened the first official McDonald's franchise in 1955 in Des Plaines, Illinois. It took a while for the golden arches to become the symbol of fast-food royalty. Ray had to mortgage his home and even sell his Multimixer milkshake machines to keep things afloat.

Fast forward to the '60s and '70s, and McDonald's was not just a local joint; it was taking over the world. Ray's persistence to turn a small idea into something colossal paid off. He embraced every opportunity that came his way and transformed McDonald's into the global giant we know today. So, what's the takeaway from Ray Kroc's story? Persistence and opportunity make an unstoppable team. Ray's determination to turn a local burger joint into an international empire is a prime example of how the combination of grit and recognizing the right opportunities can lead to something truly extraordinary. It is not just a success story; it is a lesson in turning a dream into a worldwide legacy.

Cultivating the Spirit of Perseverance

Have you ever found yourself wondering about the untapped reservoirs of perseverance within you? Ask yourself this: What dreams or goals have you set aside because the path seemed too tough? Now, picture this: You, standing at the peak of a mountain, the result of every step, stumble and climb. Imagine the satisfaction, the sense of accomplishment. The truth is, cultivating the spirit of perseverance is not reserved for a select few; it is a garden you can start tending at any point in life. All it takes is a realization that each effort, each setback, is a seed planted and a commitment to your cause. Whether you are at the foot of the mountain or halfway up, the journey of perseverance begins with that first step, that first decision to keep going. It is completely within your grasp, waiting for you to recognize the strength you hold and the heights you can reach.

Start with your Mindset

"Life's not about how hard of a hit you can give... it is about how many you can take and still keep moving forward."

- Sylvester Stallone

This quote sets the stage for understanding the power of a growth mindset in staying resilient and persistent. Imagine your mind as a mighty engine fueled by the belief that your abilities and intelligence can be developed with time and effort-this is what we call a growth mindset. When your mind is fixated on growth, it works like a built-in compass pointing you toward progress. You do not just stick to the path; you become the path. Challenges and setbacks become stepping stones rather than roadblocks. Falling down is just a brief pause; getting up is a reflex because you know each stumble is a lesson, not a failure.

Now, imagine having this growth mindset in your arsenal. It is not about being the smartest or the most talented; it is about believing that you can become better through effort and perseverance. Challenges become exciting puzzles to solve, and setbacks are merely temporary detours on your journey to success. So, here is a thought for you: What if, just like Musk, Oprah, and Bezos, you cultivated this growth mindset? What if you approached each obstacle as a chance to learn and grow? The journey becomes not just about reaching a destination but about becoming the person capable of achieving it.

Shake off the Fear of Failure

As Winston Churchill wisely put it, "Success is stumbling from failure to failure with no loss of enthusiasm." Now, let's talk about a crucial step in cultivating perseverance: shedding the fear of failure. Think about it this way: have you ever learned to ride a bike without a couple of falls? Embracing failure is like acknowledging the training wheels on the bike of life. Statistics tell us that some of the most successful people have faced failures numerous times. Michael Jordan, for instance, missed over 9,000 shots in his career! The point is failures are not roadblocks; they are the stepping stones to growth. They teach us more than our successes ever could. So, when you stumble, take it not as a sign to give up but as a blessing in disguise, guiding you toward resilience and eventual success. Remember, every fall is a lesson, and every lesson is a step forward on the path of perseverance.

Become 1 % Better Every Day.

Imagine this: What if, instead of aiming for giant leaps, you committed to becoming just 1% better every day? This approach is the embodiment of the growth mindset we have been talking about. Setting unrealistic goals can feel like trying to eat an elephant in one go-daunting and perhaps not the best idea. But focusing on that 1% improvement daily? That's like having bite-sized portions, manageable and doable. It is not about instant transformation but a steady, consistent climb. Picture it as climbing stairs-each step, no matter how small, gets you closer to the top. In a year, you will be 365% better than when you started! You end up learning new skills, leaving failures behind, and carrying forward valuable lessons. So, why not make it a goal to become just 1% better each day? It is a compound interest for your personal growth and the results might just surprise you.

Be Open to Risks

Taking risks might sound a bit scary, but let me tell you, by learning to take risks, you up the chances of facing more challenging situations. It is a bit like leveling up in a game with risks, tougher challenges, and bigger rewards. Picture this: Jeff Bezos, the brain behind Amazon, once took a massive leap of faith into the unknown world of e-commerce. His risk turned out to be the catalyst for transforming an online bookstore into the retail giant we know today. It is not just about the risk; it is about what you do when things get tricky. Adaptation becomes your superpower. As the saying goes, "Life is either a daring adventure or nothing at all." So, why not take a cue from the risk-takers? Embrace those challenges, adapt, and watch yourself grow into a leader of your own story. Ready for the adventure?

Get out of the Zone of Resistance:

Have you ever experienced that feeling of discomfort, fear, and doubt every time you plan to make a big move? That's the zone of resistance, my friend. It is this mental space where our brains throw up a barricade, kind of like a "Proceed with Caution" sign. But here is the deal: understanding this resistance is like figuring out the secret code to unlock your potential. It is a psychological barrier that often stops us from doing incredible things in life. Once you recognize it, you are already on the path to breaking it down. Picture it like a fortress, and every small step you take toward your goals is like chipping away at the walls. So, the next time you feel that resistance kicking in, take a deep breath, acknowledge it, and then take that one small step.

Use the 40% Percent Rule.

When your mind is screaming, "I'm done, I cannot do this," guess what? You are only 40% done. Wrap your head around that! Our minds are like a mix of cheerleader and party pooper. The 40% rule is your reminder that when you hit that wall of exhaustion, there is a hidden stash of energy and determination waiting to be unleashed. So, here is the deal: start applying the 40% rule in your life. The next time your brain tries to convince you to throw in the towel, remember you have got that extra 60% waiting to kick in. It is not just a physical thing; it is a mindset shift. You apply this, and voila, you are on your way to developing the spirit of perseverance.

Flex Your Muscles and Flex Your Mind

search shows that regular exercise boosts your mental strength big time. Studies reveal that people who exercise regularly tend to show higher levels of resilience and determination. When you make sweating a part of your routine, you are not just toning those muscles; you are toning your perseverance, too. So, here is the deal: incorporate daily exercise into your life. It is not just about getting fit; it is about building that mental muscle for resilience. Trust me, you will be blown away by the changes you will see in yourself.

Focus on the "WHY"

You set out on a journey, be it a project, a career, or a personal goal. It is exciting at first, right? But then, hurdles show up, challenges throw punches, and suddenly, it is like you are in the ring with life. In those moments, here is your secret weapon: remember your "why." Why did you start this in the first place? What fueled your ambition? That burning desire is your compass, your North Star. Keep that "why" at the forefront of your mind. So, when the going gets tough, remember your goals and ambitions. Let that "why" echo in your ears, and watch how it fuels your endurance in the face of anything. You have got this!

Have a Network of Support

"Surround yourself with the dreamers and the doers, the believers, and thinkers, but most of all, surround yourself with those who see the greatness within you, even when you do not see it yourself." Building a solid support network is like having your personal cheerleading squad for the journey of perseverance. The people around you influence your mindset, so why not have the right influences? Connect with people who have that growth mindset, who radiate positivity and watch how it charges up your own mind. With the right crew, you break free from the chains of fear and doubt. You learn to take risks, fight through the challenges, and emerge stronger. So, build that supportive network. Surround yourself with the ones who believe in your greatness. Together, you will conquer the highs and lows of life's obstacle course.

Set Clear Targets

Picture your journey to success-it is like a marathon, right? Now, setting clear benchmarks is like planting little flags along the route. These are checkpoints that remind you of the ground you have covered. So, why do this? Well, success is not an overnight gig; it is a journey with twists, turns, and maybe a few detours. Now, imagine this: you hit a benchmark and bam! You treat yourself to fancy lunch, new clothes, or a weekend getaway, whatever floats your boat. It is a pit stop to recharge. These rewards are not just treats; they are fuel for your perseverance engine. When times get tough, and you are eyeing that next benchmark, the promise of a reward keeps you motivated. It is like having your personal cheerleader saying, "You are doing great; keep going!" So, set those benchmarks, enjoy the rewards, and let them be your motivation boosters on the journey to success.

Chapter 5
Unwavering Faith in Oneself:

As the saying goes, "**Believe you can, and you are halfway there**." These wise words by Theodore Roosevelt hold a powerful truth, especially when it comes to stepping into the world of entrepreneurship. Faith in yourself is like the cornerstone of building your dreams. Here is the deal: when you believe in your capabilities, when you have that unwavering faith that you can navigate the challenges, you are already halfway to achieving your dreams. Entrepreneurship is a journey filled with uncertainties, risks, and the unknown. But here is where faith becomes your compass. It is that inner voice saying, "I have got this." When you trust yourself, you are more likely to take bold steps, overcome obstacles, and turn challenges into opportunities. So, faith is not just a warm fuzzy feeling; it is a driving force that propels you forward on the path to realizing your dreams in the entrepreneurial arena. It is the fuel that keeps you going when the road gets tough. Embrace that faith in yourself and watch how it transforms your entrepreneurial journey.

"Our self-assurance in trusting our abilities, capacities, and judgments; the belief that we can meet the demands of a task."

Chris Gardner, though perhaps less widely known than some high-profile figures, is a testament to the transformative impact of self-belief and perseverance. Gardner faced immense challenges early in life, including homelessness while raising his young son. Undeterred by the difficulties, Gardner clung to his belief that he could create a better life for himself and his child. While facing homelessness, Gardner secured an internship at a prestigious stock brokerage firm despite having no financial background. His relentless determination and self-belief enabled him to endure the hardships of balancing an unpaid internship with the challenges of homelessness. Gardner's story became the inspiration for the film "The Pursuit of Happiness," starring Will Smith.

Through his unwavering faith in his own potential and an unyielding work ethic, Gardner eventually became a successful stockbroker, author, and motivational speaker. His journey from homelessness to success illustrates the profound impact of maintaining faith in oneself, even in the face of seemingly insurmountable obstacles. Gardner's story resonates with many individuals striving to overcome adversity and pursue their dreams, demonstrating that personal belief can be the catalyst for transformative change.

So, what self-belief really means? Imagine looking in the mirror and genuinely thinking, "I have got what it takes to tackle whatever comes my way." Here is what self-belief does to you:

You Feel Good About Yourself: Self-belief is all about feeling good about who you are. When you have strong self-belief, you see yourself as capable and worthy. It has this positive vibe that says, "I deserve success, and I can handle whatever life throws at me."

You Call the Shots Internally: People with solid self-belief often feel like they are in control of their lives. They see their successes and setbacks as a result of their own efforts and choices, not just luck or external stuff.

You Strive Through Tough Times: A big part of self-belief is being able to bounce back when things get tough. Instead of seeing challenges as roadblocks, you view them as chances to grow. It is that resilience that helps you push through setbacks and stay motivated.

You Take Risks and Get Stuff Done: Self-belief encourages you to take risks and be proactive. You are more likely to step out of your comfort zone, explore new opportunities, and face challenges head-on. It is that feeling of "I have got this" that pushes you to make things happen.

You Make Smart Decisions: When you trust in yourself, decision-making becomes more straightforward. You are more likely to make choices based on a realistic understanding of your skills. This empowerment leads to a sense of control over the outcomes of your decisions.

You Set and Crush Goals: Self-belief is like the secret sauce for setting and achieving goals. With confidence in your abilities, you are more likely to aim high and actually hit those targets. Your belief in yourself becomes the fuel that keeps you going.

Your Performance Is Boosted: Psychology tells us that self-belief can seriously impact how well you perform. It is like a self-fulfilling prophecy-when you believe in yourself, and you tend to do better because that confidence positively influences your actions.

It Offers Mental and Emotional Perks: Building self-belief is not just about actions; it brings some mental and emotional perks too. Less anxiety, more motivation, and an overall sense of well-being-like a package deal that boosts your mental and emotional strength.

In my early 20s, I found myself at rock bottom, grappling with low self-esteem and a sense of purposelessness. It was a challenging phase, and I struggled to envision a way out.

During that challenging, there was a specific incident that served as a wake-up call, highlighting the importance of self-belief. I had an opportunity to pursue a passion project that aligned with my deepest aspirations. However, my pervasive self-doubt almost led me to decline the opportunity, convinced that I was not capable of success. In a moment of reflection, I recognized the self-sabotaging nature of my thoughts. It dawned on me that my lack of belief was the primary obstacle preventing me from seizing potentially life-changing opportunities. That realization became a turning point, prompting me to go on a journey of self-discovery and empowerment.

I started incorporating daily affirmations, reminding myself of my capabilities and worth. As I gradually embraced a more positive mindset, I noticed a remarkable shift. The passion project I initially hesitated to pursue began to flourish, opening doors to new possibilities and affirming the profound impact of self-belief.

Establishing Self-belief

External factors, whether criticism, setbacks, or comparisons, can cast doubt on our abilities and potential. But here is the thing: believing in ourselves is a continuous process. It is similar to tending to a garden; we need to water and nurture our self-belief regularly. Just as plants grow with care and attention, our confidence and self-assurance flourish when we consistently invest in them. So, when doubt creeps in, remember that reaffirming our faith in ourselves is an ongoing commitment. It is about recognizing the external influences, acknowledging them, and then actively choosing to reinforce our belief in our capabilities. Like a resilient plant, our self-belief can weather storms and thrive with a bit of mindful nurturing.

Clarify Your Aspirations

When grappling with self-doubt or succumbing to self-pity, it is crucial to envision the person you aspire to become. Ask yourself, if fear were not a factor, what actions would you take? This initial step is pivotal in the journey to restore your self-belief because doubts and negative thought patterns can bury your true self alongside your aspirations. To foster self-belief, actively pursue these aspirations while warding off feelings of low self-esteem. Take a moment to dream freely and compile a list of your goals and aspirations. As you engage in this process, confront self-doubts head-on and dismiss them, gradually crafting a comprehensive list that embodies your beliefs.

Affirm & Reaffirm Yourself

Affirmations serve as powerful tools, reinforcing our self-belief by influencing our self-perception and subsequent behavior. If we visualize ourselves as confident, capable individuals, our actions tend to reflect that self-assuredness. For instance, envisioning oneself as a future CEO fosters behaviors aligned with leadership and ambition. Creating a positive self-image is crucial, and affirmations play a key role in crafting this perception. These affirmations uttered aloud with conviction, dismantle doubts and solidify a positive self-view. Consider these affirmations:

"I am worthy of all my aspirations."

"I possess the intelligence to reach my goals."

"I deserve the finest life has to offer."

"I commit daily effort toward specific desires and goals for a fulfilling life."

Create a concise list of affirmations, stand before a mirror, and recite these phrases to yourself. It need not be lengthy-just four uplifting sentences can empower you to embrace each day with confidence and determination.

Challenge your Fears

A potent method to cultivate self-belief involves confronting your fears, but it is important not to overwhelm yourself by tackling everything at once or diving straight into the most intimidating challenge. Start gradually by identifying the root cause of your self-doubt and addressing it. For instance, if childhood experiences have shaken your confidence, consider initiating a conversation with your parents about it. Do not fear their reaction; expressing your feelings might alleviate the weight you have carried for so long.

Following this, confront the fear of potential failure in achieving your aspirations. Attend that job interview or present your innovative ideas to the board of directors. If a relationship consistently undermines your self-esteem, muster the courage to walk away. By courageously facing and triumphing over these fears, you will witness a gradual departure of self-doubt, making space for burgeoning self-belief.

Shush Your Inner Critic

To reaffirm self-belief, it is essential to address and quieten your inner critic, especially if it is the primary source of your self-doubt. Unlike external factors like societal influences, the internal voice of self-criticism requires intentional efforts to be silenced. Often, the lack of self-belief stems from an overly active inner critic, a relentless voice that questions the validity of your ideas or capabilities. For instance, you might doubt the worthiness of your brilliant proposal, convincing yourself it is inadequate and discarding it.

Confronting your inner critic is pivotal because, until you do, you risk continuously undermining your abilities and settling for less than you deserve. When your inner critic questions, "Why would they pick me for the job?" counteract it by asking, "Why should not they pick me for the job?" Proceed to enumerate all the reasons that qualify you for the position. Repeating this process will gradually silence your inner critic, fostering significant growth in your self-belief.

Inspire Others

Did you know that uplifting others can reshape your perspective on success? Often, a decline in self-belief may extend to doubting the capabilities of others. You might unknowingly discourage people from pursuing their dreams due to your own skepticism. Actively view success as attainable by anyone and make a conscious effort to encourage friends and family. Over time, this positive outlook will reflect inward, motivating you to pursue your own goals.

Prioritize Self-Care

Nurturing self-belief involves more than just mental and emotional care-physical well-being plays a crucial role in influencing mental health. Treat yourself to a spa day and indulge in a massage, shop for outfits that boost your confidence, and invest in personal grooming. Joining a gym, maintaining a healthy diet, and ensuring adequate rest are also vital. Seek support from a therapist or a support group. Looking and feeling good contribute significantly to enhancing self-confidence.

Avoid Negative Influences

Terminate associations with so-called friends who undermine your worth through words or actions, as their presence can thwart your efforts to rebuild self-esteem. Regardless of the relationship, cutting off individuals who contribute to feelings of unworthiness is crucial. If family members are the source of negativity, address the issue directly and communicate your intolerance for negativity. In cases of abusive partners, sever ties to allow room for your self-belief to flourish. While distancing from negative influences, strengthen bonds with supportive friends and family to cultivate positive relationships.

Tales of Self-assured Entrepreneurs

Countless entrepreneurial success stories stand as a testament to the profound impact of unwavering faith in oneself and one's ideas. From tech moguls to fashion trailblazers, these individuals went on paths fraught with challenges, skepticism, and uncertainties. Yet, their steadfast belief in their vision propelled them forward.

Richard Branson: Elevating Dreams to the Skies

Sir Richard Branson, the British business magnate and founder of the Virgin Group, is a living testament to the transformative power of self-belief. Born on July 18, 1950, in Surrey, England, Branson displayed entrepreneurial flair from an early age. At 16, he started Student magazine, foreshadowing a career marked by audacious ventures.

In 1970, Branson founded Virgin as a mail-order record retailer. With a bold vision and unwavering self-belief, he expanded Virgin Records, signing iconic artists like the Sex Pistols and creating the Virgin brand synonymous with innovation and quality. Branson's belief in challenging the status quo led Virgin into diverse industries, from airlines to telecommunications. Virgin Atlantic Airways, launched in 1984, defied skepticism in an industry dominated by established players. Branson's self-belief and commitment to delivering exceptional customer experiences positioned Virgin Atlantic as a major player in the airline industry.

The Virgin brand continued to diversify, encompassing Virgin Mobile, Virgin Trains, and Virgin Galactic, a commercial spaceflight venture. Despite facing setbacks, such as the challenges in the early days of Virgin Galactic, Branson's unyielding self-belief in the potential for space tourism and exploration propelled the company to achieve significant milestones. Throughout his career, Branson's adventurous spirit and belief in the power of business to drive positive change have been evident. He has embraced challenges, taken risks, and demonstrated resilience in the face of failures. Branson's life story underscores how self-belief, combined with a willingness to innovate and take calculated risks, can lead to remarkable achievements and global influence. Sir Richard Branson's journey from a mail-order record retailer to a space entrepreneur reflects the extraordinary heights that self-belief can help one reach.

Arianna Huffington: Media Maven and Thrive Global Founder

Arianna Huffington, the Greek-American author, columnist, and businesswoman, serves as a compelling example of self-belief leading to significant achievements. Born on July 15, 1950, in Athens, Greece, Huffington's journey is characterized by her resilience, diverse career, and the founding of Thrive Global, a wellness and productivity platform.

Huffington initially gained recognition as a conservative commentator and author, but it was her foray into digital media that solidified her impact. In 2005, she co-founded The Huffington Post, an online news and blog platform which became one of the most visited news websites globally. Despite initial skepticism from traditional media outlets, Huffington's belief in the power of online journalism and citizen contributors propelled The Huffington Post to success.

Later in her career, Arianna Huffington turned her attention to well-being and productivity. In 2016, she founded Thrive Global, a company dedicated to addressing burnout and enhancing mental resilience in the workplace. This endeavor reflected her belief in the importance of prioritizing well-being in our fast-paced, digitally-driven world. Arianna Huffington's story showcases the dynamic evolution of a self-assured individual who not only excelled in traditional media but also pioneered a shift toward digital journalism and wellness advocacy, demonstrating the profound impact of self-belief on personal and professional accomplishments.

The Role of Confidence in Achieving Dreams

Confidence is the linchpin of success, a sentiment emphasized by the World Economic Forum, which contends that without confidence, a significant portion of one's competence remains untapped. This underscores the critical relationship between confidence and realizing one's true potential. Building confidence is a cyclical process: setting and achieving goals bolsters confidence, yet it takes confidence to establish ambitious goals in the first place.

The challenge lies in combating the negative voices within our minds, often referred to as the "negative committee." These internal voices, though normal, can sabotage confidence and impede success. Numerous studies confirm that confidence is a more influential predictor of success than competence. Therefore, dismissing the negative committee becomes imperative. Ann Bradford's advice to tell them to "sit down and shut up" underscores the need to take charge of our thoughts.

Overcoming negative self-talk requires deliberate effort, akin to dealing with any entity working against organizational goals. By dismissing the negative committee, one can pave the way for renewed self-confidence. The intertwining relationship between confidence and success is evident; setting and achieving goals increases confidence, while confidence is a prerequisite for setting the right goals.

What happens when you are not confident?

When you are talented and passionate about your dreams but lack confidence, it is much like having a powerful engine without the key to start it. This lack of confidence can be a silent roadblock, keeping you from pursuing what you love. Imagine a musician who's a virtuoso in private but never steps on stage due to stage fright. This fear of taking risks, facing potential failures, or even the fear of success itself can hinder progress. Confidence acts as the fuel that propels your talents into action. It is not about being boastful but having the belief in your abilities, acknowledging your worth and embracing challenges. Confidence transforms that hesitant musician into a performer who captivates audiences, turning potential into reality. It shapes your mindset, helping you navigate obstacles, seize opportunities, and present your talents to the world with assurance. It is the key that unlocks the door to your dreams and says, "I am capable, and I am ready."

After a recent seminar on tech innovation, I had the pleasure of meeting Olivia, an aspiring tech innovator brimming with brilliant ideas.

Her vision for a revolutionary app was nothing short of groundbreaking. The way she spoke about reshaping the tech landscape with her exceptional coding skills was truly inspiring. However, as our conversation unfolded, it became clear that Olivia's extraordinary ideas were held captive by a lack of confidence. She hesitated to pitch her concepts to investors or assemble a team, paralyzed by the fear of criticism and self-doubt about her leadership capabilities. It was disheartening to witness such untapped potential as her transformative ideas remained dormant, waiting for the key of confidence to unlock their true impact on the world.

In my career, I have encountered numerous young and immensely talented individuals brimming with passion and groundbreaking ideas. However, what often holds them back from realizing their full potential is a conspicuous lack of confidence. Witnessing these brilliant minds stifled by self-doubt, unable to fully embrace their innovative ideas or pursue their dreams, has been a driving force behind my emphasis on the power of confidence in achieving success. It has become evident that confidence, when combined with passion and great ideas, forms a triumphant trio essential for unlocking one's true potential and making a lasting impact.

How is Confidence Linked to Entrepreneurial Success?

"Believe you can, and you are halfway there." -Theodore Roosevelt

Starting a business is an exciting and challenging journey that needs a special set of skills and qualities. Studies over the years have shown that successful entrepreneurs share certain characteristics. Among these, having confidence in yourself is the most important. Confidence serves as the guiding force that empowers entrepreneurs to embrace calculated risks and navigate uncharted territories. In the face of uncertainties, the courage instilled by confidence becomes a key factor in making crucial decisions that can shape the trajectory of their entrepreneurial journey.

Contagious Influence on Business Relationships:

Confidence is not merely a personal attribute; it possesses a contagious quality that profoundly influences how entrepreneurs are perceived and engaged with in the business realm. Interacting with investors, partners, or customers, a confident entrepreneur serves as a beacon of trust and credibility. This influence forms the bedrock of positive and enduring business relationships, creating an environment conducive to collaboration and mutual success.

Resilience in the Face of Setbacks:

The entrepreneurial journey is fraught with challenges, setbacks, and inevitable failures. Confidence, acting as a protective shield, equips entrepreneurs with the resilience needed to weather these storms. In the face of adversities, confident entrepreneurs exhibit a remarkable ability to bounce back, extracting valuable insights from setbacks and persisting with unwavering determination. This resilience becomes a linchpin for overcoming obstacles and adapting to the dynamic nature of the business landscape.

Thinking positively is a big part of having self-confidence. When entrepreneurs have a positive attitude, they develop a mindset that sees possibilities and believes in good outcomes. This positive thinking is like a boost for coming up with new ideas, solving problems, and being strong when things get challenging. And it is not just good for the entrepreneur – it also inspires people around them and attracts new opportunities.

Enhancing Communication for Effective Leadership:

Effective communication stands as a cornerstone of entrepreneurial triumph. Confidence emerges as a key player in this arena, empowering entrepreneurs to articulate their vision with persuasiveness and clarity. Whether communicating ideas, persuading stakeholders, or leading teams, a confident entrepreneur fosters an environment of inspiration and collaboration. This ability to convey a compelling vision enhances leadership effectiveness, creating a motivated and cohesive team aligned with the entrepreneurial goals.

Taking Action and Not Giving Up

Having self-confidence is great, but it needs to be backed up with action. Entrepreneurs have to take steps toward their goals, and they need to keep going, no matter what. Even when faced with problems, they keep trying, finding smart solutions, and changing their plans if needed. Being persistent is the key to overcoming challenges and turning problems into chances to grow. Entrepreneurs need to stay true to their vision, always trying to get better at what they do.

Keys to Building Unwavering Faith

It is this incredible belief in yourself that acts as your strongest armor. In your personal life, having unshakable confidence helps you navigate through tough times with grace, knowing you have what it takes to handle anything that comes your way. Professionally, having a powerful engine driving you forward always assures that you can reach those big dreams and turn challenges into opportunities. This steadfast belief in yourself is like having a sturdy foundation – it keeps you grounded, resilient, and ready to conquer any challenge life throws at you.

Do you often wonder whether you have the same unwavering faith and belief in yourself as the people we have made big in this world? Well, here is a set of some questions that you can answer honestly and assess your level of self-belief. Knowing how much you believe in yourself will help you realize how much do you need to work on your self-belief and make it unshakable.

- Do I embrace challenges?
- Am I willing to take on new challenges, or do I often shy away from them?
- How do I react when faced with setbacks or obstacles?
- Am I setting and pursuing goals?
- Do I set realistic and achievable goals for myself?
- How committed am I to pursuing and achieving those goals?
- How do I handle criticism?
- Do I take constructive criticism as an opportunity to learn and grow?
- Does negative feedback significantly affect my self-confidence?
- What's my internal dialogue like?

- Do I catch myself thinking positively or often find negative thoughts dominating my mind?
- How do I speak to myself during challenging times?
- Do I celebrate my achievements?
- Do I acknowledge and celebrate my successes, no matter how small?
- Am I quick to dismiss my accomplishments or downplay their significance?
- How do I handle uncertainty?
- Do I have a fear of the unknown, or am I open to embracing uncertainty?
- How comfortable am I with taking calculated risks?
- What's my response to the comparison?
- Do I find myself frequently comparing my journey to others?
- How does comparing myself to others affect my self-esteem?
- Am I continuously learning and growing?
- Do I actively seek opportunities for personal and professional development?
- How comfortable am I stepping out of my comfort zone to learn new things?
- How do I treat myself during challenges?
- Do I practice self-compassion and kindness during difficult times?
- Am I patient with myself when things do not go as planned?
- What's my vision for the future?

- Do I have a clear vision of where I want to go in life?

- How strongly do I believe in my ability to turn that vision into reality?

What did you find about yourself? Was it something you already knew or an eye-opening revelation? Knowing yourself, your key strengths, and your weaknesses also opens doors to confidence. Here are some key factors that can help unlock deeper levels of self-awareness:

Know Your Strengths

As the famous author Marcus Buckingham said, "Discover what you do not like doing and stop doing it." Ever thought about your strengths being like a guiding compass to boost your self-belief? It is a secret map for your abilities, those skills, talents, and unique qualities you excel in. Knowing these strengths is not just about recognizing what you are good at; it is a confidence booster. For instance, let's say you are great at problem-solving. When challenges come up, knowing this strength is like relying on a trusted tool in your toolkit, giving you the confidence to navigate any situation. Think about shifting your focus from dwelling on weaknesses to spotlighting achievements and capabilities. If you are a pro at communication, acknowledging this strength means you are less likely to be bogged down by doubts. You feel more assured, especially in situations where effective communication is crucial.

And that resilience you cultivate through knowing your strengths? Imagine you are adaptable; challenges become opportunities for learning and growth. This resilience becomes a cornerstone of your self-belief, helping you confidently navigate tough times. Being aware of your strengths also helps you set realistic and achievable goals. Tailoring objectives based on your natural strengths allows you to accomplish those goals. For example, if you are organized, you can effectively streamline your work process by setting and achieving realistic goals, reinforcing your belief in your capabilities.

Develop Your Skills:

Continuous learning is the key to unlocking unwavering faith. Albert Einstein once said, "Intellectual growth should commence at birth and cease only at death." Confidence and developing skills go hand in hand, creating a kind of teamwork that helps us grow personally and professionally. Imagine confidence and skill development as a team that cheers each other on. When you learn new things and gain skills, it boosts your confidence. And when your confidence gets a boost, you are more motivated to keep learning and improving your skills.

Confidence is like a friend that encourages you to take risks and try new things. Learning new skills often involves facing challenges and stepping out of your comfort zone. If you are confident, you are more likely to take on these challenges, even if they seem a bit scary. It is the belief that you can handle the unknown and come out stronger. The more skills you acquire, the more competent you become. Competence is like a magnet for confidence. When you know you have the knowledge and abilities to tackle tasks efficiently, your confidence naturally gets a boost. It is a bit like knowing you have the tools in your toolkit to handle any job that comes your way.

For instance, In the current digital landscape, acquiring digital marketing skills is a valuable asset for personal and professional development. Digital marketing involves leveraging online platforms and tools to connect with audiences effectively. Learning the ropes of social media marketing, search engine optimization (SEO), and content marketing is like unlocking the keys to a dynamic and ever-expanding realm. It empowers you to create engaging online content, optimize websites for visibility, and navigate the intricacies of promoting products or services in the digital space. Whether you are an entrepreneur, a professional looking to advance in your career, or someone exploring the digital landscape, learning digital marketing skills is akin to gaining a versatile toolkit.

Set Reasonable Goals:

The age-old wisdom, "A journey of a thousand miles begins with a single step," encapsulates the essence of breaking down substantial dreams into manageable tasks. Picture your big aspirations as a distant destination and the achievable goals as the individual steps leading you there. By dissecting your grand vision into smaller, doable tasks, you transform what might seem like an overwhelming journey into a series of manageable strides. Each completed task becomes a stepping stone, a tangible accomplishment that propels you forward. This incremental progress acts as a powerful motivator, creating a positive feedback loop. The more you achieve, the more your confidence grows. It is akin to stacking stones in a path - with each addition, the pathway becomes more defined, and your belief in your ability to navigate it becomes stronger.

This deliberate process not only keeps you motivated but also cultivates a robust belief in your capabilities. It shifts your focus from the enormity of the end goal to the tangible and achievable steps right in front of you. With each small victory, you are not only inching closer to your overarching dream but also building a reservoir of self-assurance. It is a journey where every accomplished goal becomes a testament to your capability, reinforcing the unwavering faith that you have what it takes to reach the summit.

Stop Comparing Yourself to Others:

Words by Theodore Roosevelt, "Comparison is the thief of joy," succinctly capture the detrimental impact of measuring your journey against that of others. Each individual's path is inherently unique, influenced by a myriad of factors that make direct comparisons an apples-to-oranges exercise.

Redirecting your focus to your own progress becomes paramount in building unwavering faith in your capabilities and journey. Rather than fixating on external benchmarks or the perceived achievements of others, nurturing a deep awareness of your own growth and accomplishments proves more fruitful.

Celebrating your victories, no matter how small, becomes a cornerstone of fostering unwavering faith. These personal triumphs are like milestones, markers that highlight your progress and reinforce your belief in what you can achieve. Simultaneously, learning from challenges becomes a constructive process when approached without the burden of comparison. It is about viewing setbacks not as reflections of inadequacy but as opportunities for growth and refinement, much like a sculptor chiseling away imperfections to reveal the masterpiece within.

Accept Who You Are:

At the core of unwavering faith lies the profound act of accepting yourself, a sentiment beautifully expressed by poet Maya Angelou: "If you are always trying to be normal, you will never know how amazing you can be." This wisdom underscores the importance of embracing your authentic self, quirks, imperfections, and all. It is a recognition that true confidence and self-belief can only flourish when grounded in self-acceptance.

The journey toward self-acceptance is a liberating acknowledgment that you are a unique and constantly evolving individual. Instead of conforming to societal expectations or a preconceived notion of "normal," you allow yourself to be authentically you. It is akin to stepping into the fullness of your own identity, acknowledging that your individuality is not a flaw but a source of strength.

Embracing your uniqueness becomes a powerful catalyst for building unwavering faith. Rather than seeing differences as shortcomings, you begin to recognize them as threads in the rich tapestry of your character. Your quirks become distinctive features that make you extraordinary, and your imperfections become stepping stones for growth and self-improvement.

The acceptance of being a work in progress further enhances your confidence. It is an admission that, like everyone else, you are on a continuous journey of self-discovery and development. This acknowledgment does not diminish your worth; instead, it amplifies it by allowing room for improvement, resilience, and the pursuit of becoming the best version of yourself.

Be Kind to Yourself:

Extending kindness to yourself is akin to a soothing breeze that tenderly nurtures the seeds of faith within. It involves adopting a compassionate and understanding approach towards your own journey, treating yourself with the same warmth and empathy you would readily offer to a friend. This perspective recognizes that, much like nature, growth requires patience, care, and acceptance of both sunny days and stormy nights.

In the landscape of personal development, mistakes and setbacks are integral aspects of the journey, not indicators of failure. This mindset reframes challenges as opportunities for learning and growth, acknowledging that missteps are not roadblocks but rather stepping stones. The analogy of being both a masterpiece and a work in progress simultaneously captures this essence - a reminder that your inherent worth is not contingent upon perfection but thrives amidst the continuous process of becoming.

The gentle kindness you extend to yourself creates a nurturing environment for the seeds of faith to sprout and flourish. It is an acknowledgment that, just like any living thing, you require nourishment, care, and understanding. This self-compassion becomes a source of resilience, allowing you to weather the storms of life with a sense of inner peace and confidence.

Moreover, treating yourself with kindness is an affirmation of your worthiness. It rejects the notion of harsh self-criticism and embraces the understanding that, despite imperfections, you are deserving of love and understanding. In the same way you would encourage a friend during challenging times, being kind to yourself involves offering words of encouragement, acknowledging progress, and celebrating victories, no matter how small.

Challenging Yourself:

Visualize challenges as the weights you lift at the mental gym, sculpting and strengthening your mental muscles. Eleanor Roosevelt's timeless wisdom encapsulates this notion perfectly: "Do one thing every day that scares you." The idea is to view each challenge as an opportunity for growth and self-discovery, akin to lifting heavier weights to build physical strength.

Stepping out of your comfort zone is like venturing into uncharted territories. It is in these spaces of discomfort and uncertainty that you encounter challenges that might initially seem daunting. However, much like lifting weights that initially feel heavy, facing these challenges becomes a deliberate exercise in resilience and mental fortitude.

Pushing your limits is not about seeking discomfort for its own sake but about expanding the boundaries of what you believe is possible. Just as you progressively increase the weight at the gym to challenge your muscles, confronting increasingly complex challenges stretches your mental capacity. This intentional stretching fosters a sense of resilience -

the ability to bounce back from setbacks and face future challenges with greater confidence.

Create a Powerful Vision:

Think of a clear vision as a reliable compass that illuminates your path through the dense fog of uncertainty. Helen Keller's profound words echo this sentiment: "The only thing worse than being blind is having sight but no vision." In this analogy, your vision serves as a beacon, a guiding light that not only allows you to see but also imparts direction and purpose to your journey.

Much like a compass point north, your vision serves as your North Star, a constant reference point in the ever-changing landscape of life. It provides a clear sense of where you want to go and what you aim to achieve. Without a vision, it is akin to exploring through thick fog without a compass - you might have the ability to see, but the lack of direction can lead to wandering aimlessly.

A powerful vision acts as a magnetic force, pulling you forward with focus and determination. It becomes the driving force behind your actions, decisions, and goals. When faced with challenges or distractions, your vision serves as a reminder of the bigger picture, helping you stay steadfast on your chosen path.

Increase Competence:

Imagine competence as the powerful engine propelling the vehicle of unwavering faith. Zig Ziglar's motivational wisdom encapsulates this idea perfectly: "You do not have to be great to start, but you have to start to be great." In this analogy, competence is not an innate quality but a dynamic force that is cultivated through learning, experience, and the courage to begin.

Picture your journey as a vehicle going through the twists and turns of life. Competence acts as the engine, providing the necessary energy and propulsion. Just as an engine is crucial for the functioning of a vehicle, competence is essential for the development and sustenance of unwavering faith. It is the tangible proof of your abilities and skills, the driving force that moves you forward.

The notion that you do not have to be great from the outset but must take that first step reflects the importance of initiation. Competence is built over time, often starting with small, deliberate actions. It is the accumulation of knowledge, the refinement of skills, and the honing of your craft through consistent effort and practice.

Building competence becomes a transformative journey. As you acquire new skills and deepen your understanding, your belief in your abilities solidifies. It is a self-reinforcing cycle where the more competent you become, the more confident you feel. This growing confidence, in turn, fuels your unwavering faith in your capacity to navigate challenges and achieve your goals.

Chapter 6
Transformative Power of Dreams and Action:

"Keep your dreams alive. Understand to achieve anything requires faith and belief in yourself, vision, hard work, determination, and dedication. Remember, all things are possible for those who believe."

- Gail Devers

As a financial specialist, I have witnessed the transformative power of dreams coupled with action in the entrepreneurial realm. Matteo was a budding entrepreneur with a dream of revolutionizing sustainable technology when I first met him after a conference in Milan. His vision was bold, but at the outset, it seemed daunting. However, Matteo did not let the enormity of his dream deter him. He meticulously crafted a business plan, seeking funding and support from like-minded individuals. Despite initial rejections and setbacks, he persisted.

Matteo's unwavering belief in his dream drove him to take actionable steps every day. He networked, researched, and fine-tuned his business model. He learned from failures and used them as stepping stones toward success. Eventually, his dedication paid off. He secured investors who believed in his vision. His sustainable technology company took shape, making strides in the industry.

The transformative power here lies not just in Matteo's dream but in his consistent action toward realizing it. Dreams without action remain mere wishes. It is the fusion of ambition with tangible, strategic steps that actualize the vision. In the entrepreneurial world, dreams are the catalysts, but action is the engine that propels those dreams toward reality.

Dreams infuse passion and purpose, igniting the entrepreneurial spirit. However, it is the deliberate, persistent actions that convert these dreams into tangible achievements. Entrepreneurs must marry their aspirations with practical steps – crafting business plans, seeking mentorship, securing funding, and adapting to market dynamics.

The synergy between dreams and action is profound. Dreams set the direction, inspiring innovation and driving ambition. Meanwhile, action fuels progress, overcoming obstacles and turning visions into viable businesses. This transformative duo not only shapes the entrepreneurial journey but also creates enduring impacts in the financial realm.

Dreams as the Catalyst for Change

When actions are not backed by dreams, you risk wandering without purpose. Your endeavors may lack a clear direction and guiding vision, leading to a series of disconnected and potentially futile efforts. Dreams provide the motivation and inspiration that drive strategic actions. Without them, you might find yourself in a cycle of short-term, reactive decision-making rather than pursuing a cohesive, long-term vision. I have seen how dreams act as the compass for successful entrepreneurs, steering them toward meaningful goals and sustainable financial success. So, don't just take action for the sake of it; ensure every step is aligned with a compelling dream that fuels your passion and purpose in the entrepreneurial landscape.

1. Passion as a Driving Force: Passion is the emotional fuel that drives entrepreneurs to pursue their dreams. It is the intense enthusiasm and commitment to an idea that propels individuals to overcome obstacles and stay dedicated to their goals. Passionate entrepreneurs find intrinsic motivation in their work, making the entrepreneurial journey more fulfilling and sustainable. This emotional connection to the dream not only sustains the entrepreneur through challenges but also positively impacts the work environment, fostering creativity and resilience.

2. Inspiring Others: A passionate entrepreneur radiates enthusiasm, and this energy can be contagious. A compelling vision, backed by genuine passion, inspires and attracts others to join the journey. Team members, investors, and customers are drawn to the sincerity and commitment of a leader who is driven by a powerful dream. This shared sense of purpose creates a cohesive and motivated team, aligning everyone toward a common goal. It transforms the business from a mere venture into a collective endeavor that resonates with a broader community.

3. Continuous Learning and Adaptation: Dreams inherently involve a vision of the future, and achieving that vision requires staying ahead of the curve. Entrepreneurs with a dream are naturally inclined towards continuous learning. They seek knowledge, stay informed about industry trends, and adapt their strategies based on evolving circumstances. This adaptability is a key factor in exploring the dynamic and ever-changing landscape of business, ensuring that the business remains relevant and competitive.

4. Balancing Realism and Ambition: While passion and dreams provide the drive, successful entrepreneurs also understand the importance of grounding their ambitions in reality. Balancing realism with ambition calls for setting achievable goals, understanding market dynamics, assessing available resources, and recognizing potential challenges. This pragmatic approach ensures that the pursuit of the dream is guided by practical considerations, increasing the likelihood of sustainable success.

5. Celebrating Milestones: The entrepreneurial journey is a series of milestones, and celebrating these achievements is really important for morale and motivation. Whether big or small, each milestone represents progress toward the dream. Recognizing and celebrating these moments not only provides a sense of accomplishment but also energizes the entrepreneur and the team. It reinforces the belief that the dream is attainable and instills confidence for the challenges ahead.

6. Risk-Taking and Courage: Dreams often involve stepping into the unknown, and realizing them requires a willingness to take calculated risks. Entrepreneurs driven by a strong vision exhibit courage by embracing uncertainty, experimenting with new ideas, and challenging the status quo. This risk-taking mentality is essential for innovation and growth, distinguishing dream-driven entrepreneurs from those who shy away from change.

7. Long-Term Sustainability: A well-defined dream acts as a guiding star for long-term sustainability. It helps entrepreneurs make decisions that align with the overarching vision, preventing short-sighted choices that may compromise the business's longevity. Sustainability goes beyond financial stability and includes the ability to adapt to market shifts, changing consumer preferences, and emerging technologies, all of which are essential considerations for a business with a lasting impact.

8. Ethical Considerations: Dreams often reflect not only the financial goals of entrepreneurs but also their values and principles. Entrepreneurs with a strong vision tend to prioritize ethical considerations, shaping the culture of their businesses. This commitment to ethical practices enhances brand reputation and fosters customer loyalty. The alignment of business decisions with ethical values not only contributes to the positive impact of the business on society but also creates a more sustainable and trusted brand.

Self-Awareness in the Entrepreneur Journey

Jumping into the entrepreneurial game without a good dose of awareness is like trying to find your way in a maze with your eyes closed – total chaos! It is like driving blindfolded and hoping you don't crash. Without awareness, you are basically stumbling around in the dark, possibly missing out on sweet opportunities or crashing into unexpected challenges. Picture it as wandering through a pitch-black room, where you are more likely to stub your toe on something or miss finding hidden treasures. Having your radar on during this entrepreneurial ride is like turning on the lights in that dark room. It helps you spot obstacles, grab opportunities and stay on top of the game. So, it is not just about having a killer idea; it is about keeping your eyes peeled, being alert to what's happening around you, and being flexible enough to roll with the punches in the crazy world of entrepreneurship.

The Mirror of Self-Discovery

Imagine the mirror of self-discovery as your entrepreneurial crystal ball. It is like this magical tool that gives you a front-row seat to your own journey. So, grab that mirror and take a good look. It reflects not just your dazzling wins but also your messy hair days – the mistakes, the pitfalls, and the challenges you faced. It is your personal reality check. Now, here is the deal on how to use it: first off, be brave and stare into it. Embrace the good, the bad, and the ugly. It is your raw material. Next, analyze what you see. What worked? What flopped? This mirror helps you spot patterns and learn from your own story. It is like a highlight reel of your entrepreneurial adventures. Take a moment to celebrate victories, but also face the not-so-great stuff head-on.

A year and a half ago, I met Jake. He was a go-getter with a killer business idea that could revolutionize the fitness industry. He envisioned an app that seamlessly blended workout plans with nutritional advice, a one-stop-shop for fitness enthusiasts. However, Jake's downfall wasn't the idea – it was his lack of self-awareness. Sure, he was passionate and driven, but he did not take the time to understand his own strengths and weaknesses. Jake believed he could handle everything, from coding the app to marketing it. The result? A tangled mess of unfinished tasks and missed deadlines.

Despite his determination, Jake struggled with coding intricacies, and marketing was like going through uncharted territory for him. His lack of awareness about his own limitations led to burnout and a half-baked product. If only Jake had taken a step back, recognized his strengths (the visionary aspect and passion for fitness), and sought help or collaborated with those skilled in areas where he lacked expertise, his entrepreneurial journey could have been a success story. Unfortunately, his lack of self-awareness became the stumbling block that prevented his brilliant business idea from reaching its full potential. The takeaway here? Know thyself before diving headfirst into the entrepreneurial sea.

The Visibility Maze

Think of visibility as your financial fingerprint – unique to your business and essential for attracting investors or customers. To traverse the maze successfully, you have got to master the art of financial storytelling. Numbers are not just figures; they are your business narrative. Clearly articulate your revenue streams, expenses, and profit margins. This transparency builds trust and gives stakeholders a roadmap of your financial journey.

Now, let's talk about the magic words: financial projections. It is like a crystal ball but for business. Break down your revenue forecasts, expense projections, and cash flow estimates. It is not about having a crystal-clear vision of the future (let's be real, who does?) but demonstrating a well-thought-out plan. This not only reassures potential investors but also guides your own financial decisions.

Next stop! risk management. The visibility maze is full of unexpected turns, and financial specialists know it is not about avoiding risks but understanding and mitigating them. Identify the financial risks specific to your venture and showcase strategies to tackle them. It is like showing that you are not just driving blindly but have a GPS for potential financial pitfalls. Lastly, remember the power of financial transparency. Don't hide behind spreadsheets – bring your numbers to life. Whether it is in investor pitches or marketing materials, make your financial story accessible and easy to understand. This not only attracts investors but also resonates with customers who want to know they are investing in a financially sound business.

In essence, for wannabe entrepreneurs, the Visibility Maze is an opportunity rather than a hurdle. From a financial standpoint, it is about embracing your numbers, projecting wisely, managing risks, and being transparent. Mastering this financial dance will not only make you more attractive to investors but will also help you navigate the entrepreneurial landscape with confidence.

Matching Your Offer to Market Needs

Have you clearly defined your target market? It is not about casting a wide net; it is about learning about the specific needs and preferences of the audience you are aiming to serve. Who are they? What are their pain points? Tailoring your offer to their requirements is like hitting the bullseye. Now, let's dive into the financial aspect. Have you conducted a cost analysis? Understanding the financial viability of your offer is key. What are the production costs, and how do they align with what your target market is willing to pay? A thorough cost assessment ensures that your pricing is competitive and sustainable.

Speaking of pricing, have you considered the perceived value of your offer? It is not just about the numbers; it is about how your target market perceives the worth of what you are offering. What unique value does your product or service bring to the table, and is it reflected in your pricing strategy? Let's talk about scalability. Have you assessed the scalability of your business model? Matching your offer to market needs requires not just meeting current demands but being poised for growth. Can your financial structure accommodate an increase in production or service delivery if demand surges?

Risk management is another critical point. Have you identified potential financial risks associated with your offer? Understanding the risks allows you to develop strategies to mitigate them. Whether it is market fluctuations or unforeseen expenses, being financially prepared is your safety net. Lastly, have you tested your offer in the market? Sometimes, what looks good on paper may need adjustments when exposed to the real world. Conduct pilot programs, gather feedback, and be ready to adapt your financial strategy based on the market's response.

I encourage you to dig deep, crunch the numbers, and ensure that your financial strategy aligns seamlessly with the evolving needs of your target market.

Overcoming the 'Selling to Everyone' Fallacy

Back in the day, I had this groundbreaking product I believed everyone needed. So, I cast a wide net, marketing it to everyone and anyone. The result? Sure, there was some buzz, but the costs skyrocketed, and the profits were barely a blip on the radar. Now, let's talk about financial sense. From a specialist standpoint, the 'Selling to Everyone' fallacy can be a costly affair. Imagine investing heavily in marketing campaigns, product variations, and distribution channels without a clear target audience. It is like throwing money into a black hole. Defining a specific target customer is not just about focus; it is about financial efficiency. Your resources are limited, and targeting everyone dilutes your message, drains your budget, and weakens your market position. Instead, identify a niche – a group with a genuine need for your product – and tailor your strategies.

1. **Resource Efficiency:** Resources, especially in the early stages, are limited. From a financial standpoint, targeting everyone is akin to spreading yourself too thin. It leads to a dispersion of marketing budgets, dilution of messaging, and inefficiencies in product development and distribution.

2. **Message Clarity:** Trying to appeal to everyone results in a diluted and generic message. This lack of specificity makes it challenging for potential customers to resonate with your brand. A focused, clear message tailored to a specific target audience ensures better communication and engagement.

3. **Cost Management:** The costs associated with marketing, product development, and distribution can quickly escalate when attempting to reach a broad audience. Defining a target customer allows for a more strategic allocation of resources, reducing

unnecessary expenditures and maximizing the impact of every dollar spent.

4. **Market Positioning:** In a crowded marketplace, differentiation is crucial. By targeting a specific audience, you can tailor your product to meet their unique needs, thereby carving out a niche market position. This specialization enhances the perceived value of your product or service.

5. **Return on Investment (ROI):** Financial success is not just about revenue; it is about profitability. Focusing on a target customer allows for a more precise measurement of ROI. It ensures that your marketing efforts generate meaningful leads and conversions, translating into a higher return on your investment.

Refining the Approach: Instead of falling into the 'Selling to Everyone' fallacy, aspiring entrepreneurs should embrace a more strategic approach:

1. **Identify a Niche:** Pinpoint a specific group with a genuine need for your product. Understand their demographics, preferences, and pain points. This niche becomes the focal point of your marketing and product development efforts.

2. **Tailor Strategies:** Develop targeted marketing campaigns that resonate with your identified niche. Tailor your product or service to meet the specific requirements of this audience. Personalization enhances customer satisfaction and loyalty.

3. **Priority Marketing Channels:** Focus your marketing efforts on channels where your target audience is most active. Whether it is social media platforms, industry events, or niche publications, prioritize channels that offer the highest likelihood of reaching and engaging with your desired customer base.

4. **Iterative Approach:** Continuously gather feedback and data from your target audience. Use this information to refine your strategies and product offerings. An iterative approach ensures that you stay aligned with your audience's evolving needs.

The Art of Positioning

How well do you stand out in a crowd of competitors? That's what positioning is all about. Have you clearly identified your unique value proposition in the market? It is not just about what you offer but how you position it financially. Have you examined your pricing strategy concerning your competitors? Understanding their pricing and where you stand can be a game-changer. Now, let's talk costs. Have you optimized your cost structure to support your positioning? Whether it is offering premium quality or a budget-friendly option, your financial setup should align with your chosen position. Lastly, have you factored in the financial implications of your chosen position on marketing and brand building? Positioning is not just about perception; it is about how you financially sustain and reinforce that position in the market. So, think about how your financial decisions support and amplify the unique spot you aim to claim in your industry—it is the financial backbone of your strategic position.

Cultivating Buyer Awareness

Think of it this way: your product or service might be the next big thing, but if no one knows about it, what's the point? Building buyer awareness is not just about popularity; it is a financial investment with tangible returns. When potential customers are aware of your brand, it translates to increased sales and revenue. This awareness doesn't happen by magic; it requires strategic and, yes, financial efforts. Marketing campaigns, advertising, and brand-building activities all play a role, and they need budgetary backing. Creating a buzz around your business not only attracts customers but also adds value to your brand, potentially allowing you to command premium prices. So, aspiring entrepreneurs, remember that cultivating buyer awareness is not just a marketing buzzword – it is a financial strategy that pays dividends in the long run. Invest wisely and watch your brand awareness transform into financial success!

Meet Lily, an aspiring entrepreneur who has developed a line of eco-friendly, reusable household products. To cultivate buyer awareness, Lily starts by investing in a well-thought-out marketing campaign. She leverages social media platforms, influencers, and eco-conscious communities to spread the word about her sustainable products. This campaign includes engaging content, informative blog posts, and eye-catching visuals that highlight the environmental benefits of her products.

Lily also collaborates with like-minded businesses and participates in relevant events and trade shows to showcase her products. To sweeten the deal, she offers limited-time promotions and discounts to early adopters. Additionally, Lily ensures her online presence is strong, with an easy-to-navigate website and an active presence on e-commerce platforms.

From a financial standpoint, Lily allocates a portion of her budget to advertising, influencer partnerships, and promotional activities. She carefully tracks the return on investment (ROI) from these initiatives, analyzing the impact on website traffic, sales conversions, and customer feedback. Over time, Lily's consistent efforts in cultivating buyer awareness pay off as her brand gains recognition, customer loyalty grows, and her eco-friendly products become a sought-after choice in the market. This example underscores the financial importance of strategic awareness-building efforts for a budding entrepreneur.

Bridging the Self-Awareness Gap

In the early days, fueled by enthusiasm, I delved headfirst into launching a business without fully understanding my strengths and weaknesses. The result? Despite pouring countless hours and resources, the venture struggled to gain traction. It was a humbling experience that prompted me to explore the realm of self-awareness.

I started by reflecting on my past endeavors, seeking candid feedback from mentors and peers, and embracing the uncomfortable but enlightening process of understanding my own motivations and limitations. This introspective journey led to a remarkable shift. Armed with a newfound understanding of my skills, values, and areas needing improvement, subsequent entrepreneurial ventures were marked by strategic decisions, targeted efforts, and a more authentic leadership approach. Bridging the self-awareness gap is a really important journey for wannabe entrepreneurs. Here is a guide to help you navigate this path effectively:

- Reflect on Strengths and Weaknesses: Take a deep dive into your skill set, experiences, and areas where you excel. Equally important is recognizing your weaknesses. This introspection lays the foundation for understanding your capabilities and areas that may need improvement.

- Seeking Feedback: Don't hesitate to request input from mentors, colleagues, or friends. External perspectives offer valuable insights into blind spots and aspects you might not have considered. Constructive criticism is a really important tool for personal and professional growth.

- Assessing Values and Motivations: Understand your core values and motivations. What propels you beyond financial success? Aligning your entrepreneurial journey with your values ensures a more fulfilling and purpose-driven pursuit.

- Embracing Failure as a Learning Opportunity: Failure is an inevitable aspect of the entrepreneurial journey. Instead of perceiving it negatively, view it as an opportunity to learn. Analyze your failures, comprehend what went wrong, and leverage these insights to adapt and grow.

- Using Personality Assessments: Consider undertaking personality assessments such as the Myers-Briggs Type Indicator

(MBTI) or StrengthsFinder. These tools offer structured insights into your personality, preferences, and strengths, enhancing your self-understanding.

- Setting Clear Goals: Define both short-term and long-term goals for your entrepreneurial venture. These goals serve as a compass, directing your actions and decisions and providing clarity and direction toward your desired destination.

- Prioritizing Self-Care: Entrepreneurship can be demanding, both mentally and physically. Prioritize self-care to maintain a healthy balance. Ensure sufficient sleep, exercise, and moments of relaxation. A well-nurtured self is more resilient and self-aware.

- Engaging in Regular Reflection: Dedicate time regularly for self-reflection. Journaling or meditation can be effective tools for gaining clarity on your thoughts, emotions, and aspirations. Regular reflection fosters continuous self-awareness.

- Cultivating Emotional Intelligence: Understand and manage your emotions effectively. Emotional intelligence plays a significant role in interpersonal relationships, decision-making, and leadership. It is a key component of self-awareness.

- Building a Support Network: Surround yourself with a supportive network of mentors, peers, and friends. Engage in open and honest conversations about your strengths and areas for improvement. Constructive feedback from your network can be invaluable.

- Invest in Learning: Stay curious and invest in continuous learning. Attend workshops and conferences or enroll in courses that align with your interests and goals. Learning expands your knowledge base and enhances your self-awareness.

Targeted Selling

It is not just about casting a wide net; it is about hitting the bullseye and here is why it is crucial. When you tailor your selling efforts to a specific audience, you are not just saving money; you are investing it wisely. Focused selling enables you to allocate your resources towards connecting with individuals most inclined to purchase your product or service, thereby optimizing your return on investment. Explore avenues such as targeted social media advertising, employing specific demographic parameters, crafting email marketing initiatives customized for segmented customer lists, or collaborating with influencers who resonate with your niche audience. By comprehending and narrowing down the needs and preferences of your target market, you not only enhance the efficiency of your sales endeavors but also ensure that each dollar spent stands a better chance of converting into revenue. Therefore, aspiring business leaders, take note: in the realm of finance, targeted selling is not merely a strategy but a shrewd financial move that propels your entrepreneurial aspirations closer to fruition.

Jumping Over Tasks

When entrepreneurs fail to jump over tasks, essentially meaning they are not completing projects but instead juggling multiple endeavors simultaneously, it can lead to significant setbacks. Imagine trying to build a house by laying a brick here, then rushing to another spot and starting another without finishing the first. The result? A lot of unfinished structures and no completed homes. Similarly, for business owners, tackling multiple projects at once can lead to a lack of focus and productivity and ultimately hinder success. The marketplace is noisy and filled with distractions, trends, and competitors. Without a clear and actionable plan, startups can easily be swayed off course, spreading themselves thin across various initiatives.

To overcome this, it is really important to design projects with actionable and achievable milestones. Break down tasks into manageable chunks, set realistic deadlines, and complete one before moving on to the next. This not only ensures a sense of accomplishment but also allows for a more focused and strategic approach. By completing projects one step at a time, entrepreneurs can navigate the marketplace noise with clarity, making progress and achieving success in a more sustainable manner.

The Pitfall of Multitasking

As the saying goes, "The man who chases two rabbits catches neither." This wise quote encapsulates the pitfall of multitasking, a trap many entrepreneurs fall into. Imagine a chef trying to simultaneously cook five different dishes – the result would likely be a chaotic mess rather than a gourmet meal. Similarly, entrepreneurs who multitask and do not focus on one single project can find themselves in a tangled web of incomplete tasks, missed deadlines, and compromised quality. Instead of excelling in one area, they risk spreading themselves too thin, diminishing their effectiveness across the board. Multitasking not only hampers productivity but can also lead to increased stress, decreased attention to detail, and a lack of innovation. To avoid this pitfall, successful entrepreneurs prioritize tasks, focusing on one project at a time, achieving milestones and ensuring a higher quality output.

Dealing with the Market Noise

Shutting out market noise is vital for entrepreneurs to maintain focus, make informed decisions, and foster business growth. In the bustling marketplace, there is a constant barrage of trends, opinions, and external pressures that can easily lead entrepreneurs astray. By shutting out the noise, entrepreneurs create a mental space to concentrate on their unique vision and business objectives. This clarity is essential for strategic planning and effective decision-making. Constant exposure to market noise can create unnecessary distractions, fostering a reactive rather than proactive approach to business. Entrepreneurs need to stay attuned to their own goals and customer needs rather than being swayed by every passing trend. Ultimately, shutting out market noise allows entrepreneurs to cultivate a resilient and authentic business strategy, fostering long-term success.

Consider a small, local coffee shop as an example. Instead of constantly chasing the latest marketing gimmicks or rapidly changing social media trends, the owner decides to focus on building a strong local community presence. They invest in personalized customer experiences, engage with the community through events and sponsorships, and consistently deliver high-quality products. While competitors may be caught up in the noise of viral marketing trends, the coffee shop's steady and authentic approach builds lasting customer relationships and a solid local reputation. By avoiding the noise and concentrating on a targeted, community-centric strategy, the coffee shop thrives amidst the ever-changing marketing landscape.

Single-Tasking for Success

As the saying goes, "Do one thing every day that scares you." This quote by Eleanor Roosevelt highlights the courage and focus required to achieve success, which aligns with the importance of single-tasking for entrepreneurs. Imagine an entrepreneur who decides to single-task on a new product launch. Instead of dividing her attention among various projects, she dedicates her time, energy, and resources solely to this venture. By focusing on one task at a time, Sarah can delve deeply into market research, perfect the product, and execute a targeted marketing strategy. The result is a well-crafted, thoroughly planned product launch that stands out in the market. Single-tasking allows entrepreneurs to bring their full creative and analytical power to a specific project, fostering innovation, quality, and, ultimately, success. It minimizes the risk of burnout, improves productivity, and ensures that each endeavor receives the attention and dedication it deserves.

Milestones Matter

"Success is not final. Failure is not fatal: It is the courage to continue that count."

- Winston S. Churchill

This quote underscores the significance of continuous progress, and that's where the concept of milestones comes into play for entrepreneurs. Each milestone becomes a stepping stone, guiding the way forward. For instance, successfully securing seed funding is not just a financial win but also a validation of the business concept. Milestones matter because they provide a roadmap, helping entrepreneurs measure progress, make informed decisions, and build resilience on the entrepreneurial journey. They transform the pursuit of success into a series of manageable and meaningful steps, fostering a mindset of continuous improvement.

Avoiding the Overcommitment Trap

You are a wannabe entrepreneur with a head full of ideas and a heart full of passion. The danger? The over-commitment trap. It is an illusion that you can do it all – launch multiple businesses, juggle countless projects simultaneously, and wear every hat in the entrepreneurial circus. But let me tell you, it is a trap that can lead to burnout, subpar results, and even the demise of your ventures. To avoid the overcommitment trap, start by acknowledging your limits. Understand that time and energy are finite resources. Prioritize your projects based on feasibility, market demand, and personal capacity. It is imperative to set realistic goals and timelines, focusing on quality over quantity. Learn to say no to opportunities that don't align with your core objectives.

Additionally, build a solid support system. Surround yourself with a reliable team or seek mentorship to share the load. Delegating tasks allows you to concentrate on your strengths and prevents the dilution of effort across too many fronts. Lastly, embrace the power of strategic planning. Break down your projects into manageable phases with clear milestones. This not only helps in tracking progress but also prevents the feeling of drowning in an endless sea of tasks. Remember, success in entrepreneurship is not about doing everything; it is about doing the right things well. So, steer clear of the overcommitment trap by staying focused, setting realistic expectations, and building a strong foundation for your entrepreneurial journey.

Learn how to work a process

Think of a process as your trusted guide, built on principles that lead to victory. It is not just about having a plan; it is about diving in and putting in the daily grind. While having a plan is foundational, the true essence lies in the willingness to dive into the intricacies of execution. It entails a disciplined and persistent approach, navigating challenges and seizing opportunities on a day-to-day basis. The process becomes the trusted companion on the journey, offering a structured framework that not only propels progress but also instills a sense of purpose and discipline essential for overcoming obstacles and achieving victory in the long run. Here is your roadmap:

Get the Core Principle:

Every process has a rock-solid principle behind it. Identify that principle – it could be anything from killer marketing to top-notch customer service. That's your North Star. In the world of entrepreneurship, every successful process is built on a fundamental principle that serves as its guiding force. This principle encapsulates the essence of what makes the process effective. It could be a commitment to innovation, an unwavering focus on customer satisfaction, or a dedication to delivering unmatched quality. Identifying this core principle is akin to finding your North Star – it provides direction, purpose, and a clear path forward.

One standout example is the late Steve Jobs, co-founder of Apple Inc. His core principle was relentless innovation. Jobs believed in pushing the boundaries of technology and design to create revolutionary products that would reshape industries. From the Macintosh to the iPhone, Apple's success has been grounded in the core principle of delivering cutting-edge, user-friendly technology. This commitment to innovation not only set Apple apart in the market but also created a brand synonymous with quality and forward-thinking.

Jobs' dedication to this core principle was evident in Apple's product launches, marketing strategies, and company culture. The principle of innovation guided every aspect of the business, making it a beacon for both customers and competitors. By staying true to this North Star, Steve Jobs and Apple became pioneers in the tech industry, showcasing the transformative power of identifying and adhering to a core principle in the entrepreneurial journey.

Be Mr./Ms. Consistent:

Once you know the principle, commit to being consistent. Processes are like habits; the more you repeat, the more they shape success. It is not a one-time thing; it is a way of life. Consistency is the backbone of success in entrepreneurship. Once you have identified the core principle that drives your process, the next crucial step is to commit to consistency. Processes, much like habits, are strengthened through repetition. Consistency is not a one-time effort but rather a way of life – a commitment to applying the principle consistently over the long term.

Warren Buffett, the legendary investor and CEO of Berkshire Hathaway, exemplifies the power of consistency in the application of principles. Buffett's core principle is value investing. He identified early in his career that the key to successful investing lies in identifying undervalued companies with strong fundamentals and holding onto them for the long term.

Buffett's commitment to the principle of value investing is marked by unwavering consistency. He did not chase short-term market trends or succumb to the pressure of quick gains. Instead, he patiently applied the same principle of seeking undervalued opportunities over decades. This consistency became a way of life for Buffett and played a pivotal role in his extraordinary success. By sticking to the principle of value investing through market ups and downs, Buffett built a reputation for sound decision-making and achieved remarkable wealth. His disciplined and consistent approach serves as a powerful reminder that success in entrepreneurship often hinges on the commitment to consistently applying core principles over time.

Tap into Resources:

Use all the tools in your arsenal – training programs, coaching, books – to understand and embrace the process. Learn from those who have been there, done that and grab their golden nuggets of wisdom. Successful entrepreneurs often attribute their achievements to a continuous quest for knowledge and insights. They tap into various resources available to them, leveraging training programs, coaching, and books to enhance their understanding of the entrepreneurial journey. Learning from the experiences of those who have already navigated the challenges of building a business can provide invaluable guidance. One notable example is Elon Musk, the visionary entrepreneur behind companies like Tesla and SpaceX. Musk is known for his voracious reading habits and willingness to seek advice from experts in diverse fields. By assimilating knowledge from a wide range of sources, Musk has demonstrated how tapping into a rich array of resources can contribute to innovative thinking and success in the competitive business landscape. Entrepreneurs can follow this principle by actively seeking out learning opportunities and gleaning insights from the experiences of industry leaders and mentors.

Put Learning into Action:

It is not just about reading – it is about doing. Take what you learn and apply it to your hustle. Experiment, tweak, and keep refining based on what works for your unique journey. Putting learning into action is a pivotal step in the entrepreneurial journey. It is not merely about acquiring knowledge but about applying it to your endeavors. Once you have absorbed valuable insights, take proactive steps to integrate that knowledge into your business pursuits. This calls for experimentation, adaptation, and continuous refinement based on what resonates with your unique journey.

Check Your Progress:

Keep a close eye on how you are doing. Metrics and feedback are your best buds. If something's not clicking, be ready to shake things up. A process is your ally, not a rigid rulebook. For example, if your process is all about customer happiness, consistently gather feedback and tweak your offerings based on what your awesome customers are saying.

Harnessing Coaching Wisdom

What do you think is the biggest asset for someone with business aspirations? It is the mindset and education. Putting your money into education and coaching classes might feel like a splurge, especially when your funds are tight. But think of it as planting a seed that grows into a tree of knowledge, bearing fruit for a lifetime. It is not just a cost; it is an investment in your future success. The insights, skills, and guidance you pick up from education and coaching are not just quick wins – they are the gifts that keep on giving. In the fast-paced world of entrepreneurship, spending on your know-how is like buying stock in your own success story. So, don't see it as a splurge; view it as a smart move that pays off in dividends down the road. To best understand this, consider James and Hailey, both stepping into the stock market:

James is all eager to jump into the stock market without seeking guidance or education. He might believe he can figure it out as he goes along. But without understanding market dynamics, strategies and risk management, James faces challenges. No mentor or coach leads to poor decisions, losses, and frustration. James struggles to grasp buying and selling intricacies, ultimately failing to find success.

Now, consider Hailey. This individual realizes the importance of education and seeks out a mentor with stock market expertise. Hailey invests time and effort to understand the trade's tricks, learning effective strategies and gaining insights into market trends. The mentor guides Hailey, sharing practical knowledge and valuable experiences.

With this mentorship and a solid educational foundation, Hailey enters the stock market confidently. Armed with the ability to analyze stocks, manage risks, and make informed decisions, Hailey navigates the market successfully. Despite starting with less initial investment than James, Hailey's disciplined approach and mentor-guided knowledge led to substantial gains.

So, what this illustrates is that education, combined with practical guidance, is your superpower. It empowers you to make informed choices, mitigate risks, and excel in your chosen field. In the dynamic world of the stock market, mentorship becomes your crucial asset.

Reading to Realize

Reading is like having a backstage pass to the minds of successful folks who have been there, done that. It is not just about learning; it is about gaining a supercharged understanding of markets, business strategies, and personal development. Personally, I can attest to the transformative power of reading in my entrepreneurial journey. One of the financial books that left an indelible impact on me was "Rich Dad, Poor Dad" by Robert Kiyosaki. This book provided me with a paradigm shift in understanding money, assets, and investments. It prompted me to rethink my approach to wealth creation and inspired me to explore alternative income streams. Another influential read was "The Intelligent Investor" by Benjamin Graham. Graham's timeless principles of value investing became a cornerstone of my financial strategy, shaping the way I approach investment decisions. "The Alchemy of Finance" by George Soros (1994) was another great read.

These books weren't just pages of words; they were mentors who guided me through the intricate landscape of finance. The knowledge gained from reading allowed me to make more informed decisions, avoid common pitfalls, and ultimately contribute to the success of my entrepreneurial endeavors. In essence, reading serves as a compass, guiding entrepreneurs toward a deeper understanding of the markets and equipping them with the tools to navigate the complexities of business and finance.

Mindset Mechanics

Imagine your mindset as the magic wand in your journey as an entrepreneur – it is not just about what you do, but how you think that really counts. A positive mindset acts like a superhero cape, giving you the confidence to tackle challenges with a can-do attitude. Take Sara Blakely, the genius behind Spanx, for example. Despite facing numerous "no's" at the start, her positive mindset fueled her persistence, and now Spanx is a household name. Resilience is like your entrepreneurial armor, helping you bounce back when things get tough. J.K. Rowling's story echoes this – before the magic of Harry Potter, she endured rejection after rejection. Her resilient mindset turned the tables, creating the enchanting wizarding world we know today.

Lack of self-discipline

When an aspiring entrepreneur lacks self-discipline, the journey toward realizing their business ambitions becomes precarious, often marked by a series of setbacks and unfulfilled potential. Without the ability to maintain focus, adhere to schedules, and resist distractions, an entrepreneur may struggle to execute their plans effectively. For instance, consider an individual launching an e-commerce startup with a grand vision but lacking self-discipline. They may procrastinate on critical tasks, miss deadlines, and find it challenging to prioritize responsibilities. As a consequence, the business could suffer from delayed product launches, ineffective marketing strategies, and a lack of consistency in customer engagement. The absence of self-discipline not only hampers personal productivity but also jeopardizes the overall viability of the entrepreneurial venture, hindering its growth and success. In essence, self-discipline is a linchpin for an entrepreneur's ability to turn aspirations into tangible achievements.

Take the example of an aspiring entrepreneur, Jason! He is passionate about developing a mobile application that addresses a specific market need. Despite having a clear vision, he struggles with self-discipline. Instead of adhering to a structured development plan and allocating dedicated hours for coding and testing, he frequently succumbs to distractions like social media, unrelated side projects, and inconsistent work hours. As a result, the mobile app's development timeline is consistently delayed, missing crucial deadlines for beta testing and launch. The lack of self-discipline not only affects the quality of the app but also impacts potential investor interest and user engagement.

Competitors who maintain a disciplined approach in their development process may seize the market opportunity, leaving their venture at a disadvantage. In this scenario, the absence of self-discipline directly impedes the entrepreneurial journey, hindering the transformation of a promising vision into a successful and timely product.

Discipline in Decision-Making:

Consider it as the compass guiding your entrepreneurial ship. Entrepreneurship is like a maze, full of twists and turns. Discipline in decision-making is your trusty map. When faced with a multitude of choices, having a disciplined approach ensures you choose the path that aligns with your goals and vision. Envision your business as a marathon, not a sprint. Discipline in decision-making means keeping your eyes on the long-term prize. Each choice you make should contribute to the bigger picture of where you want your business to be in the future.

Every business journey has its risks, but disciplined decision-making helps you manage them smartly. It calls for weighing the pros and cons, understanding potential outcomes, and making choices that align with your risk tolerance and overall business strategy. Nobody's perfect, and mistakes are inevitable. Discipline means not just making decisions but learning from them. It is about analyzing what worked and what did not and constantly refining your decision-making process for future success. In the hustle of entrepreneurship, it is easy to lose sight of your values.

Discipline in decision-making ensures that every choice you make aligns with your core values and the mission of your business. Remember, discipline is not about being rigid; it is about being thoughtful and intentional in every decision. So, as you start your entrepreneurial journey, let discipline be your trusted companion in making choices that pave the way for success.

Product Discipline: Maintaining Quality and Innovation

Think of your product as the face of your business. Product discipline ensures that it is not just a face but a remarkable one. Consistent quality becomes your trademark, something customers remember and trust. It is the difference between a one-time purchase and a loyal customer. In the fast-paced world of entrepreneurship, standing still means falling behind. Product discipline is not just about maintaining; it is about innovating. It is the fuel that propels your business forward, keeping you ahead of the curve. Think Apple – consistently high-quality products with a dash of innovation.

Customers are the backbone of any successful business. Product discipline is your secret weapon to win their hearts. When you consistently deliver top-notch products, you build trust and loyalty. Satisfied customers become your brand advocates, spreading the word and bringing in more business. Imagine a product that never evolves. Boring, right? Product discipline means being adaptable. It is about listening to customer feedback, staying tuned to market trends, and tweaking your product to meet evolving needs. This adaptability is the key to long-term success.

Your business's reputation is gold. Product discipline safeguards it. A reputation for quality and innovation attracts not just customers but also partners and investors. It is an invaluable asset that opens doors to new opportunities. Dreaming of scaling up your business? Product discipline is your growth companion. It ensures that as your business expands, your products maintain the same level of excellence. This consistency is what fuels sustainable growth.

Action-Oriented Mindset: The Power of Disciplined Execution

Having a head full of great ideas is awesome, but an action-oriented mindset is what turns those dreams into reality. It is the difference between saying, "I want to start a business," and actually taking the steps to make it happen. Procrastination is the arch-nemesis of progress. An action-oriented mindset is your superhero cape against it. It pushes you to tackle tasks head-on, leaving no room for delays. It is about seizing the moment and making things happen.

Books and theories are fantastic, but an action-oriented mindset is about learning by doing. It is rolling up your sleeves, getting your hands dirty, and gaining real-world experience. This hands-on approach is where true entrepreneurial lessons are learned. Fear of failure can be paralyzing, but an action-oriented mindset sees failure as a stepping stone to success. It is about embracing challenges, learning from setbacks, and using them as fuel to keep moving forward.

Have you ever seen a snowball rolling down a hill, getting bigger and faster? That's what an action-oriented mindset does for your journey. Every small action builds momentum. It is about taking consistent steps that lead to significant progress over time. Whether you are a solopreneur or building a team, an action-oriented mindset sets the tone. It creates a culture where everyone is focused on getting things done. It is about setting goals, making plans, and executing them with precision.

Balancing People Skills with Business Acumen

In the business world, who you know matters as much as what you know. Navigating relationships with discipline means building a strong network. It is about connecting with people genuinely, understanding their needs, and creating mutually beneficial partnerships. Ever played the game "Telephone" as a kid? In business, miscommunication can lead to similar chaos. It calls for effective communication. It is about conveying your ideas clearly, actively listening, and ensuring everyone is on the same page.

Conflicts are inevitable, but you can resolve them gracefully. It is about finding solutions rather than pointing fingers. Mastering this skill ensures that your team stays focused on the common goal. Trust is the currency of successful relationships. It is about keeping your promises, being reliable, and building a reputation that makes people eager to work with you.

Understanding people's emotions is crucial, but so is making objective decisions. It is about being compassionate while also making decisions that benefit your business. Your team will likely have diverse backgrounds and perspectives. You can leverage this diversity. It is about recognizing the strengths each individual brings to the table and creating an environment where everyone feels valued.

A positive work environment is the breeding ground for success. It is about creating a culture where everyone feels motivated, appreciated, and encouraged to give their best. So, if you are ready to master the art of navigating relationships with discipline, you are setting the stage for a thriving business. It is not just about what you know; it is about who you know and how well you work together.

Rely on Your Potential

Imagine someone telling you that you are not cut out for business – that you lack passion, resilience, or the right look and attitude. Now, buying into these lies means letting these opinions get to you, affecting your self-esteem and confidence. It is like accepting a bad deal when you should be investing in your own success. This can seriously hinder your personal and financial growth.

But here is the financial specialist's insight: this book serves as your financial wake-up call. It is there to help you see through these lies and recognize them for what they are – roadblocks to your success. It is like getting a financial GPS to guide you away from these negative beliefs. The solution is all about realizing your true potential and identity. You are not defined by what others think about your passion, resilience, or appearance. The book is your financial roadmap, showing you that you can achieve whatever you set your mind to, even in the world of business. It is time to invest in your own success, reject the naysayers, and build your financial future with confidence and authenticity.

Shattering the Myth of Inadequacy: Overcome External Doubts

External doubts, especially in the realm of finance, can be formidable hurdles for aspiring entrepreneurs. These doubts often manifest as skepticism from others about your financial capabilities and can cast shadows on your entrepreneurial journey. Now, let's delve into practical solutions to overcome these external doubts, drawing from a financial expert's perspective.

Investing in your financial education is the foundational step. This means acquiring comprehensive knowledge about financial management, market dynamics, and industry intricacies. This expertise not only empowers you to make informed financial decisions but also establishes your credibility in financial discussions, countering external doubts. Building a robust financial network is equally crucial. Connect with mentors, advisors, and fellow entrepreneurs who have weathered similar financial challenges. This network provides valuable insights, guidance, and a supportive community that can help you navigate external doubts with confidence.

Actions indeed speak louder than words. Demonstrating your financial competence through tangible achievements is a potent antidote to external doubts. Successfully managing budgets, securing funding, or hitting financial milestones becomes irrefutable evidence of your capabilities, gradually dispelling doubts from external sources. Developing a strategic financial plan is pivotal. Outline clear financial goals, strategies, and contingency plans for your business. A well-thought-out plan not only guides your financial decisions but also communicates your commitment and foresight, acting as a shield against doubts regarding your financial acumen.

Adaptability is key in the dynamic financial landscape. Stay informed about industry trends, economic shifts, and financial innovations.

Continuous learning and adaptation not only showcase your resilience but also dispel doubts about your ability to navigate changing financial environments. Cultivating and maintaining a positive financial mindset is the linchpin. External doubts can be daunting, but viewing them as opportunities for growth rather than setbacks shifts your perspective. A positive mindset enables you to confront financial challenges with confidence and resilience, eroding doubts over time.

The Illusion of Unfitness: Recognize and Reject False Labels

"The Illusion of Unfitness" is essentially the misconception that you are not fit or capable of navigating the financial aspects of entrepreneurship. It is the false label that suggests you lack the financial acumen, skills, or innate qualities required to succeed in managing the financial side of your business.

Recognizing the Illusion: Firstly, it is really important to recognize this illusion. Often, external voices or self-doubt can contribute to this false perception. It might manifest as thoughts like "I'm not good with numbers" or "I don't have the financial background." Identifying these thoughts and understanding them as illusions is the initial step.

Dispelling the Illusion: Now, let's talk about dispelling this illusion. Recognizing that everyone starts somewhere is key. Many successful entrepreneurs did not have extensive financial backgrounds when they began. The journey calls for learning and growing.

Educational Investment: Investing in your financial education is a powerful antidote. It is never too late to enhance your financial literacy.

Attend workshops, take courses, and seek guidance from financial experts. This not only equips you with the necessary knowledge but also erodes the illusion of being unfit for financial management.

Surround Yourself with Financial Support: Build a robust financial support system. Connect with mentors, advisors, and fellow entrepreneurs who have faced similar doubts. Learning from their experiences not only provides valuable insights but also reinforces the understanding that everyone encounters challenges in their financial journey.

Prove Your Financial Competence: Take tangible steps to prove your financial competence. Implementing sound financial practices, successfully managing budgets, and hitting financial milestones serve as concrete evidence of your capabilities. It is about showcasing your skills in action and dismantling the illusion.

Strategic Financial Planning: Crafting a strategic financial plan is another essential element. Break down your financial goals into manageable steps and outline clear strategies. This not only guides your financial decisions but also showcases your commitment and capability, dispelling any doubts about your fitness in financial matters.

Redefining Entrepreneurial Identity: Craft Your Own Business Persona

Your entrepreneurial identity is essentially the persona you embody in the business world. It is how you present yourself, your values, and your approach to entrepreneurship. In the financial realm, this identity extends to how you manage money, make financial decisions, and navigate the fiscal aspects of your venture.

Crafting Your Financial Persona: When it comes to finances, crafting your entrepreneurial identity calls for defining how you interact with money. Are you a strategic planner, an innovative risk-taker, or a meticulous budgeter? Your financial persona should align with your overall entrepreneurial identity, reflecting your values and goals.

Embracing Financial Mindset: A significant part of your financial persona is your mindset. A financial expert entrepreneur doesn't just see numbers; they understand the stories they tell. Cultivate a mindset that views financial challenges as opportunities for growth and learning. This positive approach becomes a cornerstone of your financial identity.

Educational Investment in Finance: Crafting your financial persona requires an investment in your financial education. Understand the financial intricacies of your industry, learn about investment strategies, and stay updated on financial trends. This knowledge not only enhances your financial persona but also positions you as a confident and informed entrepreneur.

Aligning Financial Practices with Values: Your financial practices should align with your entrepreneurial values. If sustainability is a core value, your financial decisions should reflect that, perhaps by prioritizing eco-friendly investments. Ensuring congruence between your values and financial practices strengthens your overall entrepreneurial identity.

Building a Financial Support System: Crafting your financial persona also calls for building a robust financial support system. Connect with financial mentors, advisors, or fellow entrepreneurs who share your values and can provide guidance. This support system becomes an integral part of your financial identity, offering insights and assistance when navigating financial challenges.

Innovative Financial Strategies: As you redefine your entrepreneurial identity, consider adopting innovative financial strategies. This could involve exploring new ways of financing, leveraging technology for financial management, or creating unique revenue streams. Innovations in your financial approach contribute to a distinctive financial persona.

Adaptability in Financial Approach: The business landscape evolves, and so should your financial persona. Embrace adaptability in your financial approach. Be open to adjusting your strategies based on market trends, economic shifts, and emerging opportunities. An adaptable financial identity positions you as a resilient and forward-thinking entrepreneur.

Turning Negativity into Fuel: Harness Criticism for Motivation

In the financial realm of entrepreneurship, negativity can surface in various forms—doubts about your financial decisions, skepticism from others, or even self-criticism. Instead of letting this negativity hinder your progress, consider it an opportunity to enhance your financial acumen.

Learning from Constructive Criticism: Criticism, when constructive, is a valuable asset. It provides insights into potential pitfalls or areas for improvement in your financial strategies. As a financial expert entrepreneur, I view constructive criticism as a financial health check. Assess the validity of the feedback and use it to refine your financial approaches.

Transforming Doubts into Motivation: Negativity can be a powerful motivator if channeled correctly. As a financial expert, take any doubts or criticisms as a challenge to prove the naysayers wrong. Use the negative energy to fuel your determination to make sound financial decisions, demonstrate your competence, and achieve financial milestones.

Leveraging Financial Resilience: Financial markets can be unpredictable, and criticisms may arise during challenging times. Instead of succumbing to negativity, cultivate financial resilience. Embrace setbacks as learning opportunities, adjust your strategies based on the feedback received, and showcase adaptability in the face of financial challenges.

Seeking Financial Mentorship: Negativity can be overwhelming, especially for those starting their entrepreneurial journey. Consider seeking mentorship from seasoned financial experts. They can provide guidance, share their experiences with overcoming criticism, and offer valuable insights into exploring the financial landscape with resilience and confidence.

Focusing on Continuous Financial Improvement: Use negativity as a driving force for continuous improvement. As a financial expert entrepreneur, commit to ongoing learning and refinement of your financial skills. Embrace a growth mindset that views challenges as opportunities to elevate your financial expertise and contribute to the long-term success of your business.

Aligning Financial Goals with Personal Vision: Negativity often stems from a misalignment between personal vision and financial goals. Take a moment to reassess your financial objectives and ensure they align with your overall entrepreneurial vision. When your financial goals resonate with your broader mission, criticisms become stepping stones toward achieving your desired impact.

Celebrating Financial Milestones: Combat negativity by celebrating financial milestones, no matter how small. Recognize your achievements and use them as reminders of your financial competence. This positive reinforcement not only boosts morale but also serves as evidence that you are on the right track, counteracting negativity.

Awakening Self-Belief: Embrace Your True Entrepreneurial Spirit

Self-belief is the catalyst for building financial confidence. It is the unwavering assurance in your ability to make sound financial decisions, manage budgets effectively, and steer your business toward fiscal success. Cultivating this confidence is not just about numbers; it is about understanding the stories they tell and having faith in your capacity to interpret and navigate them.

A positive financial mindset is rooted in self-belief. As a financial expert entrepreneur, I foster a mindset that sees challenges as opportunities for growth and views setbacks as valuable lessons. This positive outlook not only influences your financial decisions but also attracts opportunities and enhances your ability to overcome financial obstacles.

Awakening self-belief calls for aligning your personal aspirations with your financial goals. Clearly define what financial success means to you and how it aligns with your broader entrepreneurial vision. This alignment creates a powerful synergy, where self-belief propels you toward your financial objectives with a sense of purpose and determination.

Self-belief doesn't shield you from setbacks; rather, it empowers you to learn and grow from them. In the financial realm, setbacks are inevitable, but with self-belief, you approach them as temporary hurdles rather than insurmountable obstacles. Extract valuable lessons from financial challenges, adjust your strategies, and move forward with renewed determination.

Self-belief thrives on knowledge. As a financial expert entrepreneur, invest in continuous financial education. Stay abreast of industry trends, financial innovations, and emerging opportunities. The more you know, the more confident and capable you become in making informed financial decisions for your business.

Building self-belief is a journey best undertaken with a supportive network. Surround yourself with mentors, advisors, and fellow entrepreneurs who believe in your potential. A supportive financial network not only provides guidance but also reinforces your self-belief during challenging financial moments.

Self-belief is strengthened by setting and achieving financial milestones. Define tangible goals, break them into manageable steps, and celebrate each accomplishment. These milestones serve as markers of your financial progress, boosting your confidence and validating your self-belief.

Chapter 7
Financial Hurdles for Startups

As Thomas Edison once said, *"I have not failed. I have just found 10,000 ways that won't work."* Similarly, in the realm of entrepreneurship, setbacks and financial hurdles are inevitable. However, it is crucial to remember that encountering obstacles doesn't equate to defeat. Instead, it is an opportunity to innovate and strategize. While the path to success may be fraught with financial challenges—be it securing funding, managing cash flow, or going through economic downturns—resilience and resourcefulness are key. Rather than succumbing to adversity, aspiring entrepreneurs must embrace it, seeking out creative solutions and leveraging available resources to overcome financial barriers. By adopting a mindset of perseverance and adaptability, entrepreneurs can transform obstacles into stepping stones on the path to building a thriving business.

Ways to fund your business idea

Say you don't have the funds you need for your startup idea. Does this mean you give up on your million-dollar idea? Absolutely not! The journey of entrepreneurship is paved with challenges, and securing funding is often a major hurdle. But worry not! There are several realistic ways to fund your business idea. From bootstrapping and seeking investment from friends and family to exploring crowdfunding platforms and pitching to angel investors or venture capitalists, the options are plentiful.

Friends and Family: Sometimes, the people closest to you can be your biggest supporters. Borrowing money from friends and family is a classic way to kickstart your business. They might just believe in your vision enough to invest in it. Just be sure to dot your i's and cross your t's legally and tread lightly to avoid any awkward Thanksgiving dinners if things don't pan out.

Small Business Loans: Banks might seem like the go-to option, but they can be a tough nut to crack for small businesses. Thankfully, there are alternative lending companies that specialize in helping entrepreneurs like you get the funds they need. Just watch out for those sneaky sharks swimming in the loan waters.

Trade Equity or Services: Who says you have to fork over cash for everything? Bartering your skills or services with fellow business owners can be a game-changer. Need some web design? Offer up your marketing expertise in return. It is a win-win... if you can find someone willing to play ball.

Bootstrapping: Sometimes, you have just gotta pull yourself up by your bootstraps (literally). Using your own funds—whether it is from your savings account, credit cards, or mortgage your home—can give you the financial freedom to get your business off the ground. Just be prepared for the possibility of some sleepless nights if things don't go as planned.

Incubator or Accelerator: Ever heard of business accelerators or incubators? They are like the Hogwarts of startups, providing communal workspaces and invaluable mentorship. Just keep in mind that they tend to favor tech-heavy businesses, so you might have to search high and low to find the perfect fit.

Crowdfunding: If you have a killer idea and a knack for social media, crowdfunding platforms like Kickstarter and Indiegogo could be your golden ticket. But beware: the competition is fierce, and you will need to drum up some serious buzz to stand out from the crowd.

Small Business Grants: If you are a woman, minority, or veteran, there might be grant money with your name on it. It is worth checking with organizations like the Small Business Administration or your local Chamber of Commerce to see if you qualify. Just be sure to read the fine print before you start celebrating.

Local Contests: Who needs Shark Tank when you have local business competitions? These contests are a great way to practice your pitch and gain exposure for your startup. Sure, you might not walk away with the top prize, but every opportunity to showcase your business is a win in our book.

Keep Your Day Job: Alright, we know this one is not the most exciting option, but hear us out. Keeping your day job while building your business on the side can provide the stability you need to weather the storm. Plus, you will gain valuable experience that will come in handy when you are ready to take the leap full-time.

Effective strategies for managing finances

By following these strategies, you can overcome financial challenges, maintain financial health, and position your business for long-term success and sustainability. It is all about setting clear goals, managing resources effectively, and making strategic decisions that support growth and profitability. With careful planning and execution, small businesses can navigate the complexities of funding and finance and thrive in today's competitive marketplace.

Strategy 1: Establish Clear Financial Goals

Setting clear financial goals is like mapping out your journey before going on a road trip. It gives you direction, purpose, and a sense of accomplishment when you hit milestones along the way. These goals serve as a roadmap, guiding small business owners and stakeholders toward success by providing clarity on where the business is heading.

- Be Specific: Define your goals with precision. Whether it is increasing revenue, improving profit margins, or expanding into new markets, clarity is key.

- Use Measurable Metrics: Identify specific metrics to track your progress. This could include revenue targets, profit margins, customer acquisition costs, or market share.

- Ensure Achievability: Set goals that are challenging yet realistic. Aim high, but make sure your goals are within reach with the resources and capabilities available to you.

- Break Down Goals: Divide larger objectives into smaller, manageable milestones. This makes them less daunting and allows for easier tracking of progress.

- Regularly Review and Adjust: Goals are not set in stone. Periodically assess your progress, adapt to changing circumstances, and adjust your goals as needed to stay on course.

Strategy 2: Create a Budget

Budgeting is the backbone of financial planning for small businesses. It is like drawing up a spending plan that ensures you are making the most of your resources and maximizing your return on investment. A well-crafted budget helps you allocate resources efficiently, prevent overspending, and identify areas where cost reductions are possible.

- Gather Financial Data: Start by collecting historical financial statements, expense records, and revenue reports. This provides a baseline for your budgeting process.

- Estimate Income: Forecast expected revenue from sales, investments, and other sources. Be realistic and conservative in your estimates to avoid overestimating income.

- List Expenses: Detail all anticipated expenses, categorizing them as fixed (e.g., rent, salaries) or variable (e.g., marketing, utilities).

- Identify Seasonal Variations: Consider any seasonal or cyclical fluctuations in income or expenses. This ensures your budget accounts for periods of high and low activity.

- Account for Contingencies: Include a contingency or emergency fund in your budget for unexpected expenses or downturns. Having a buffer ensures you are prepared for the unexpected.

- Review and Revise: Budgeting is not a one-time task—it is an ongoing process. Periodically revisit your budget, compare actual performance to your projections, and make necessary adjustments to stay on track.

Strategy 3: Monitor Cash Flow

Cash flow is the lifeblood of any business, and monitoring it closely is crucial for small businesses to maintain financial stability and sustain growth. Cash flow refers to the movement of money in and out of your business over a specific period, reflecting the net result of cash generated from sales, investments, and other sources minus expenses and financial obligations.

- Monitor Regularly: Keep a close eye on your cash flow statements and forecasts. Regular monitoring allows you to spot trends, identify potential issues, and take corrective action before they escalate.

- Invoice Promptly: Send out invoices promptly to expedite payments from customers. The faster you can convert receivables into cash, the healthier your cash flow will be.

- Offer Incentives: Encourage early payments from customers by offering discounts or other incentives. This can help improve your cash flow and strengthen customer relationships.

- Maintain Cash Reserves: Set aside emergency funds for unexpected expenses or downturns. Having a cash cushion provides financial security and peace of mind during uncertain times.

- Manage Inventory: Optimize your inventory levels to prevent excess capital from being tied up unnecessarily. Excess inventory ties up cash that could be used for other business needs.

- Negotiate Supplier Terms: Work with your suppliers to negotiate better payment terms and improve your cash flow. Extending payment terms can help you better manage your cash flow and preserve working capital.

Strategy 4: Manage Expenses Effectively

Controlling and reducing expenses is essential for small businesses to maintain financial health and sustain profitability. By managing costs efficiently, businesses can maximize their net income and ensure that revenue exceeds expenditures. This allows for day-to-day operations to continue smoothly and provides the means to invest in growth initiatives such as marketing campaigns or technology upgrades.

- Prioritize Spending: Focus on essential expenditures that directly contribute to your business objectives. Prioritize spending on activities that drive revenue or improve efficiency.

- Cut Unnecessary Costs: Regularly review your expenses and eliminate unnecessary or redundant ones. Look for opportunities to streamline processes, renegotiate contracts, or eliminate non-essential expenses.

- Negotiate with Suppliers: Negotiate better terms with your suppliers to reduce procurement costs. Explore options such as bulk discounts, volume rebates, or extended payment terms to lower your expenses.

- Implement Cost Controls: Set limits or controls on discretionary spending to prevent overspending. Establish clear guidelines and approval processes for spending to ensure expenses are aligned with your budget and business objectives.

- Use Technology: Leverage accounting software and expense management tools to streamline your financial processes and gain better control over your expenses. Automating repetitive tasks and workflows can save time and reduce errors, allowing you to focus on growing your business.

Strategy 5: Invest Wisely

Strategic investments can play a pivotal role in fueling small business growth and success. Whether it is investing in technology upgrades, marketing campaigns, staff development, or entering new markets, allocating resources wisely is essential for maximizing returns and achieving long-term objectives. Strategic investments allow businesses to innovate, expand, and gain a competitive edge in the marketplace.

- Research Thoroughly: Conduct comprehensive research to understand the industry, market, and competitors. Gather data, analyze trends, and assess the potential impact of the investment on your business.

- Assess ROI: Calculate the potential return on investment and evaluate its attractiveness. Consider factors such as revenue growth, cost savings, or improved efficiency when assessing ROI.

- Analyze Risk Factors: Identify potential risks associated with the investment, such as market volatility, competition, or regulatory changes. Evaluate the likelihood and potential impact of these risks on your business.

- Diversify Investments: Spread your investments across various opportunities to reduce risk and improve resilience. Diversification helps protect your business against unforeseen events or fluctuations in specific markets.

- Review Legal and Contractual Terms: Carefully examine contracts, agreements, and legal implications associated with the investment. Seek legal advice if necessary to ensure you fully understand the terms and obligations involved.

- Have an Exit Strategy: Plan for contingencies and establish a clear exit strategy in case the investment doesn't meet expectations. Having an exit strategy allows you to minimize losses and pivot, if necessary, to pursue alternative opportunities.

The challenges of borrowing and debt management

There are several hurdles that small businesses often face, impacting their financial health and long-term sustainability. These challenges arise from various factors and can have significant implications for the business's operations, growth prospects, and overall success.

High Interest Rates: When you do manage to borrow, you might find yourself facing higher interest rates compared to big corporations. Lenders see small businesses as riskier bets, so they often charge higher rates to cover their bases. This can drive up the cost of borrowing and make it harder to pay back what you owe.

Limited Credit History: If your business is new or hasn't borrowed much before, you might have a limited or nonexistent credit history. Lenders like to see a track record of responsible borrowing and repayment, so this can make it harder to qualify for loans or get favorable terms.

Cash Flow Constraints: Borrowing means taking on debt that needs to be repaid, which can put a strain on your cash flow. Balancing debt payments with other expenses like payroll and rent can be a juggling act, and if you are not careful, it can lead to cash flow problems down the line.

Overleveraging: Taking on too much debt relative to your business's income and resources can leave you overleveraged. This increases your financial risk and can make it tough to weather economic ups and downs or invest in growth opportunities.

Debt Service Coverage Ratio (DSCR) Requirements: Lenders often look at your Debt Service Coverage Ratio (DSCR) to assess your ability to repay debt. If your ratio is too low, it could signal trouble ahead and make it harder to get financing or refinance existing debt.

Credit Score Impact: Your borrowing and debt management decisions can impact both your personal and business credit scores. Late payments or high levels of debt can ding your credit, making it harder to borrow in the future and potentially driving up your borrowing costs.

Risk of Bankruptcy: If you are not careful, excessive debt or mismanagement could lead to bankruptcy. This can have serious consequences for your business, including the loss of assets and damage to your reputation.

So, what can you do about all of this? Well, it is all about proactive debt management and strategic financial planning. Budgeting, cash flow forecasting, and exploring alternative financing options are all good places to start. By staying on top of your finances and making smart decisions, you can navigate these challenges and set your business up for long-term success. Here are seven steps to help you manage your debt more effectively:

Take account of your accounts: It is time to face the music and make a list of all your outstanding debts. Jot down everything you owe, from credit cards to student loans. Knowing the interest rates on each debt will help you figure out which ones are hitting you the hardest.

Check your credit report: Get a hold of your credit report from one of the big three credit-reporting agencies. This will give you a clear picture of your financial standing and help you spot any errors or unrecognized accounts. Plus, it is a good way to keep tabs on your credit score.

Look for opportunities to consolidate: If you are juggling multiple high-interest loans, consolidating them into one loan with a lower interest rate could save you a bundle. Explore options like personal loans or balance transfers to get those interest rates down and make your debt more manageable.

Be honest about your spending: Take a hard look at your monthly expenses and see where you can cut back. Maybe it is time to ditch that daily latte habit or cancel that subscription you never use. Cutting expenses now will help you tackle your debt without digging yourself deeper into the hole.

Determine how much you have to pay: Once you have consolidated your debts, figure out how much you need to pay each month. Make sure this amount fits into your budget—if it doesn't, reach out to your lenders to see if you can negotiate more manageable terms.

Figure out how much extra you can budget: Take a look at your budget and see how much extra money you can throw at your debt each month. Cutting back on unnecessary expenses should free up some cash to put toward paying off those balances faster.

Determine your debt-reduction strategy: When it comes to paying off your debt, there are a couple of popular strategies to choose from. You can either focus on paying off the balances with the highest interest rates first (which will save you more money in the long run) or start with the smallest balances to build momentum and see quick progress. Whichever approach you choose, stick with it and keep chipping away at that debt!

Balance profit and investment for long-term success

Before diving into long-term investing, it is crucial to understand your current financial standing. Take stock of your assets and liabilities, including outstanding debts. Setting up a reasonable debt management plan and ensuring you have an adequate emergency fund in place will provide a solid foundation for your long-term financial goals. Taylor Schulte, a certified financial planner, compares this process to a doctor diagnosing a patient before prescribing treatment. By taking stock of your assets and debts, setting up a debt management plan, and ensuring you have an emergency fund, you are laying the groundwork for successful investing. Tackling these financial tasks first ensures that you will be able to put funds into long-term investments without needing to dip into them prematurely.

Know Your Time Horizon: Identify your investing goals and understand your time horizon. Whether it is retirement planning, saving for your children's education, or other financial objectives, knowing when you will need the funds will help determine the appropriate investment strategy and level of risk you can tolerate. For example, if you are investing in a child's college fund that is 18 years away, you may opt for a more aggressive investment strategy, knowing there is ample time to recover from market fluctuations.

Stick to Your Strategy: Once you have established your investing goals and time horizon, choose an investment strategy that aligns with your objectives and risk tolerance. Whether you prefer a conservative or aggressive approach, consistency is key. Avoid making impulsive decisions based on short-term market fluctuations, and stay committed to your long-term investment plan. Stacy Francis, president of Francis Financial, emphasizes the importance of staying committed to your strategy, even during market downturns. Having clear guidelines for your investment approach can help you weather market volatility and avoid making impulsive decisions. Whether you are investing for the short or long term, consistency is key.

Understand Investment Risks: Imagine you are planning a road trip. You have two route options: one is a straight highway with occasional traffic jams (stocks), and the other is a scenic route with winding roads and unpredictable weather (bonds). The highway may get you to your destination faster, but you might encounter delays due to traffic. On the other hand, the scenic route offers a smoother ride but takes longer to reach your destination. Similarly, stocks offer higher potential returns but come with greater volatility, while bonds provide stability but lower growth potential. By understanding these risks and your own risk tolerance, you can choose the right mix of investments to suit your financial journey.

Diversify Your Investments: Think of your investment portfolio as a garden. If you plant only one type of flower and a pest or disease affects it, your entire garden may suffer. However, if you plant a variety of flowers, some may thrive, even if others struggle. Similarly, spreading your investments across different asset classes, such as stocks, bonds, and real estate, can reduce your overall risk. Mutual funds and ETFs act like a variety pack of seeds, offering exposure to a diverse range of assets without the need for individual selection.

Mind the Costs of Investing: Consider your investment expenses, like the maintenance costs of owning a car. Just as you would shop around for the best deal on gas and insurance to minimize costs, you should be mindful of fees associated with your investments. High fees can eat into your returns over time, so it is essential to choose low-cost options whenever possible. By regularly reviewing your investment expenses and exploring alternatives, you can keep more money in your pocket and maximize your long-term gains.

Review Your Strategy Regularly: Picture yourself going through a changing landscape. As you travel, road conditions and weather patterns shift, requiring you to adjust your route and driving speed. Similarly, market conditions and personal circumstances may change over time, necessitating adjustments to your investment strategy. By conducting regular reviews of your portfolio and rebalancing as needed, you can stay on course toward your financial goals and navigate through life's twists and turns with confidence.

Chapter 8
Building a Strong Team

"Starting a business is like building a ship. You need to gather your crew, plan your voyage, and set sail into the unknown."

These wise words from media mogul Oprah Winfrey perfectly capture the essence of entrepreneurship. While securing funding is essential for launching a startup, it is equally crucial to assemble a talented and dedicated team. Investing in people who share your vision and passion can make all the difference in exploring the unpredictable waters of the business world. A strong team brings diverse skills, innovative ideas, and unwavering commitment, providing the foundation upon which your startup can thrive and weather any storm.

Finding individuals who share your vision and work ethic

Building the perfect team for your startup is paramount to laying a strong foundation for success. It's not just about hiring individuals with impressive resumes; it's about assembling a group of people who complement each other's skills, share the same passion for the company's mission, and are aligned with its values. To achieve this, startups can follow several key steps.

Define Your Company Culture and Values: Defining your company culture and values is essential to attracting individuals who align with your startup's vision and work ethic. Company culture encompasses the beliefs, behaviors, and norms that guide interactions within the organization. It reflects the company's identity, mission and how it operates on a day-to-day basis. Similarly, values represent the principles and standards that drive decision-making and behavior.

Write Clear Job Descriptions: Crafting clear and detailed job descriptions is crucial to attracting candidates who fit your startup's needs and culture. Job descriptions should clearly outline the role's responsibilities, required skills, qualifications, and expectations. Additionally, providing insights into your company culture, work environment, and benefits helps candidates gauge their fit with your organization.

Use Behavioral Interview Questions: Behavioral interview questions are effective in assessing candidates' past experiences and behaviors to predict future performance. These questions typically start with phrases like "Tell me about a time when..." and require candidates to provide specific examples of their actions and outcomes in previous situations. By focusing on concrete examples, you can gain insights into candidates' problem-solving skills, work ethic, and compatibility with your startup's culture.

Utilize Employee Referral Programs: Employee referral programs leverage your existing team's networks to attract top talent. These programs incentivize employees to refer qualified candidates for open positions within the organization. Offering rewards such as referral bonuses, recognition, or other incentives encourages employees to actively participate in the recruitment process and helps create a sense of community and engagement within the team.

Consider Remote and Flexible Work Arrangements: In today's dynamic work environment, remote and flexible work arrangements have become increasingly appealing to candidates. Offering these options can widen your talent pool and enhance employee satisfaction and productivity. Clear policies and guidelines are essential to ensure effective communication, collaboration, and performance measurement in remote and flexible work settings.

Look for Cultural Fit: Cultural fit is a critical factor in hiring individuals who share your startup's values and work ethic. Beyond skills and qualifications, assess candidates' alignment with your company culture, values, and team dynamics. Cultural fit ensures that employees feel engaged, motivated, and cohesive within the organization, contributing to overall success and productivity.

Test Candidates' Skills: Evaluating candidates' skills through various testing methods is crucial to ensure they have the capabilities required for the role. Tailor assessments to the specific job requirements and responsibilities, including written tests, practical exercises, or simulations. Fairness, objectivity, and equal opportunities for all candidates are essential considerations during the testing process.

Check References and Previous Work Experience: Thoroughly checking references and previous work experience provides insights into candidates' professional backgrounds and performance. Contacting references allows you to verify the accuracy of candidates' claims and gather additional information about their skills, work style, and contributions in previous roles. Online platforms like LinkedIn can also provide valuable insights into candidates' professional reputations and achievements.

Offer a Comprehensive Benefits Package: A comprehensive benefits package is instrumental in attracting and retaining top talent for your startup. Beyond salary, offer perks such as health insurance, retirement plans, paid time off and professional development opportunities. Customizing benefits to meet employees' needs and preferences enhances job satisfaction, morale, and overall well-being.

Create a Positive Work Environment and Company Culture: Fostering a positive work environment and company culture is essential for attracting and retaining top talent. Cultivate an inclusive, supportive, and collaborative workplace where employees feel valued, respected, and empowered to contribute their best work. Recognize and celebrate achievements, promote open communication, and prioritize employee well-being to foster a culture of positivity and success.

Creating a collaborative and supportive work environment

When team members work together cohesively towards common goals, they can achieve greater efficiency and productivity. Collaboration allows individuals to leverage each other's strengths, skills, and perspectives, leading to innovative solutions and creative problem-solving. Moreover, a supportive work environment promotes trust, respect, and open communication among team members, fostering a sense of belonging and morale. When employees feel valued and supported, they are more likely to be engaged, motivated, and committed to their work, leading to higher job satisfaction and retention rates.

Lay It All Out: Transparency is key. When companies open up about challenges and encourage employees to speak their minds, it sets the stage for a culture of trust and honesty. This openness empowers individuals to share innovative ideas and solutions without fear of judgment. Plus, when everyone's in the loop, it is easier to rally the troops and tackle any obstacles head-on.

Get Those Creative Juices Flowing: Innovation is the name of the game. By creating a safe space for brainstorming and idea-sharing, teams can tap into their collective creativity and come up with game-changing solutions. Encouraging a culture of curiosity and experimentation can lead to breakthroughs that drive the company forward.

Play to Your Strengths: Every team member brings something unique to the table. By recognizing and leveraging each person's strengths, teams can maximize their potential and achieve greater success. Whether it is through personality tests or good old-fashioned observation, understanding what makes each individual tick is essential for building a cohesive and high-performing team.

Collaboration Station: Collaboration is not just a buzzword - it is the secret sauce of successful teams. By fostering an environment where teamwork is celebrated and encouraged, companies can harness the collective intelligence of their employees to solve complex problems and achieve common goals. From cross-functional projects to informal brainstorming sessions, there are countless ways to foster collaboration and unleash the full power of the team.

Goals, Goals, Goals: Setting clear goals and expectations is essential for keeping everyone on track. When teams have a shared vision and a roadmap for success, it is easier to stay focused and motivated. Regular check-ins and progress updates help keep everyone accountable and ensure that the team is moving in the right direction. And when goals are achieved, it is cause for celebration and reflection - a chance to pat each other on the back and gear up for the next challenge.

Show Some Love: Appreciation goes a long way. By recognizing and rewarding team members for their hard work and contributions, companies can boost morale and foster a positive work environment. Whether it is through formal incentives like bonuses or promotions or simple gestures like a heartfelt thank-you note, acknowledging the efforts of individuals helps build a culture of appreciation and camaraderie.

Tech It Up a Notch: In today's digital age, technology plays a crucial role in facilitating collaboration. From video conferencing tools to project management software, there is a wide range of tech solutions available to help teams communicate, collaborate, and coordinate their efforts. By providing employees with the right tools and training, companies can streamline workflows, improve efficiency, and empower teams to do their best work.

Leadership in Entrepreneurship

You know, they say that leadership is the fuel that drives the engine of entrepreneurship. And let me tell you, that is so true! See, when you are out there chasing your dreams, trying to turn your ideas into reality, you need someone at the helm to steer the ship. That is where leadership comes in. It is about more than just calling the shots or barking orders - it is about inspiring others, making tough decisions, and charting a course through uncharted waters. A good leader knows when to take risks when to pivot, and when to rally the troops. They are the glue that holds the team together, the driving force behind every success. So, whether you are building the next big thing or just starting out on your journey, remember this: leadership is not just a title. It is a responsibility. And with great leadership, anything is possible.

Listen to Understand the Problem: Effective communication is crucial for any leader, but it is not just about speaking - it is also about listening. When you truly listen to your team members, you gain valuable insights, build trust, and foster stronger relationships. Active listening involves not only hearing what others are saying but also paying attention to their body language and emotions. By understanding the problem from different perspectives, you can develop better solutions and make more informed decisions.

Being Creative with Your Work: Creativity is not just for artists and writers; it is also a valuable asset for leaders. Creative leaders can think outside the box, anticipate challenges, and come up with innovative solutions. By encouraging creativity within your team, you can inspire fresh ideas, spark innovation, and stay ahead of the competition. Whether it is brainstorming sessions, design thinking workshops, or simply encouraging employees to take risks, fostering creativity can lead to breakthroughs and new opportunities.

Emotional Intelligence: Emotional intelligence, or EQ, is all about understanding and managing emotions - both your own and others'. Leaders with high EQ can empathize with their team members, navigate difficult conversations, and build strong relationships. By developing your emotional intelligence, you can create a more positive work environment, resolve conflicts more effectively, and motivate your team to achieve their goals.

Practice Discipline: Discipline is the foundation of effective leadership. It is about staying focused, setting priorities, and following through on your commitments. Disciplined leaders are reliable, consistent, and able to keep their teams on track. By practicing discipline in your own work habits and holding yourself accountable, you set an example for others to follow. This can help create a culture of discipline within your team, leading to greater productivity and success.

Motivate People to Grow: As a leader, one of your most important roles is to inspire and motivate your team members. This involves understanding their individual needs, goals, and aspirations and providing them with the support and encouragement they need to succeed. Whether it is offering praise and recognition, providing opportunities for professional development, or simply lending a listening ear, effective leaders can help their team members grow and thrive.

Just Keep Learning: In today's fast-paced world, learning never stops. As a leader, it is important to stay curious, open-minded, and willing to adapt to new challenges and opportunities. By continually seeking out new knowledge and experiences, you can expand your skills, stay ahead of the curve and lead your team to success. Whether it is through formal education, mentorship, or simply staying curious, the key is to keep learning and growing as a leader.

Financial Knowledge: Financial literacy is essential for any leader, especially entrepreneurs. Understanding key financial concepts like budgeting, forecasting, and cash flow management can help you make better-informed decisions and steer your business toward success. By gaining a deeper understanding of your company's financial health and performance, you can identify areas for improvement, mitigate risks, and capitalize on opportunities for growth.

Ability to Delegate: Effective delegation is a hallmark of strong leadership. By empowering your team members to take on responsibility and make decisions, you not only free up your own time but also help develop their skills and confidence. However, delegation is not just about handing off tasks - it is also about providing clear instructions, setting expectations, and offering support and feedback along the way. By mastering the art of delegation, you can build a more efficient and resilient team that can tackle challenges and seize opportunities with confidence.

Dealing with Conflicts

Conflicts are like unwelcome guests at a party. They are bound to show up uninvited, especially in the workplace. As an entrepreneur, it is crucial to recognize that conflicts are inevitable within a team setting. However, rather than seeing them as stumbling blocks, view them as opportunities for growth and improvement. Developing effective conflict management skills is essential for maintaining a cohesive and productive team environment. By honing your ability to navigate disagreements, listen to different perspectives, and facilitate constructive dialogue, you can steer your team through rough waters and emerge stronger on the other side.

Set the Stage: Establish Respect and Trust

Conflict within a startup team can be like a storm brewing on the horizon, you can see it coming, but if you are prepared, it doesn't have to wreck your ship. Start by creating an atmosphere of respect and trust among team members. Everyone should feel valued, heard, and respected. Encourage open dialogue where opinions are welcomed without fear of judgment or ridicule. When everyone feels like they are part of the conversation, conflicts are less likely to escalate.

Draw the Lines: Set Clear Boundaries

Think of boundaries like the guardrails on a highway. They keep everyone on track and prevent collisions. Make sure everyone knows what's expected of them and the consequences if they don't play by the rules. Communication is key here; don't assume everyone's on the same page. Clearly articulate roles, responsibilities, and expectations to avoid misunderstandings down the road.

Embrace the Clash: Recognize Constructive Conflict

Believe it or not, not all conflict is bad news. In fact, a little healthy debate can lead to breakthrough ideas and innovative solutions. Foster an environment where disagreements are seen as opportunities for growth rather than obstacles to be avoided. Encourage team members to challenge each other respectfully and explore different perspectives. When conflicts arise, view them as a chance to learn and improve rather than a sign of failure.

Have a Game Plan: Establish Conflict Resolution Procedures

When conflicts do rear their ugly heads (and trust me, they will), it is crucial to have a plan in place to deal with them effectively. Define a clear process for addressing conflicts, from identifying the issue to implementing a solution. Make sure all team members are aware of the protocol and feel comfortable using it. By having a roadmap for conflict resolution, you can nip problems in the bud before they spiral out of control.

Keep an Open Mind: Embracing Diversity of Thought

In the fast-paced world of startups, innovation thrives on diversity of thought. Keep an open mind and be willing to entertain ideas that challenge your own beliefs. Remember, the best solutions often come from collaboration and compromise. Encourage team members to speak up and share their perspectives, even if they differ from your own. By embracing diversity of thought, you will not only foster a more inclusive culture but also drive greater success for your startup.

Chapter 9
Market Research and Understanding Your Audience

"Know your customers and, more importantly, what they want."

- Mark Cuban

This quote succinctly captures the essence of the importance of market research and understanding your audience for startups. Conducting thorough market research allows entrepreneurs to gain valuable insights into their target market's preferences, behaviors, and pain points. By understanding their audience's needs and desires, startups can tailor their products or services to better meet customer demands, thereby increasing the likelihood of success in the competitive business landscape. Market research also helps identify market trends, potential competitors, and niche opportunities, enabling startups to make informed strategic decisions and differentiate themselves effectively.

Identify Your Niche

You know that old saying, "jack of all trades, master of none"? Well, it hits the nail on the head when it comes to carving out your own space and standing out from the crowd.

So, why is finding a niche so darn important, you ask? Buckle up because I'm about to drop some knowledge bombs on you. First off, landing on a niche helps you lock in that loyal customer base you have been dreaming of. When you cater to a specific group of people who are all about what you are offering, you are golden. They will be lining up to buy from you because they know you have got exactly what they need.

By diving deep into a niche, you are automatically dodging the big-name bullies in the market. No need to play in their sandbox when you have got your own shiny corner carved out. That means you can focus on delivering top-notch products and services without worrying about getting squashed by the big dogs.

Finding your niche can actually save you some serious dough. Say goodbye to throwing cash at broad marketing campaigns that barely hit the mark. When you know exactly who you are targeting, you can zoom in on them like a heat-seeking missile. Plus, building those personal connections with your audience? Priceless.

By becoming the go-to guru in your niche, you are not just another face in the crowd. You are the rockstar everyone's flocking to. People trust experts, plain and simple. So, why not be the one they turn to when they need what you are offering? Let's not forget about the cha-ching factor. When you are the big fish in a small pond, you can charge a pretty penny for your goods and services.

Step one: Know thy audience. Start by picking your target audience. Think about what you know, like the back of your hand, and then drill down to find those sweet subtopics. Matt Woodley suggests focusing on an area where you have got some serious know-how. Got it? Good.

Step two: Spot the gaps. Take a good hard look at your audience and check out where the market's falling short. According to Walters, your products or services should be like a soothing balm for a pain point your audience is dealing with. Find a sector that is primed for growth and jump on it.

Step three: Get to know your peeps. This one's a biggie. Walters and Woodley both swear by doing your homework on your target audience. Dive deep into their wants, needs, dreams, and gripes. Walters even suggests getting them involved from the get-go, even at the MVP stage. Keep tabs on them regularly to stay ahead of the curve.

Step four: Craft your master plan. Time to put pen to paper and map out your game plan. Woodley recommends laying it all out in a killer business plan. Define exactly what you are bringing to the table, who your dream customer is, and how you will price your goods or services. Fine-tune your idea based on what you have learned about your audience. It is all about staying laser-focused.

Step five: Spread the word. Now that you have got your niche locked down, it is time to shout it from the rooftops. Woodley's all about those targeted marketing efforts. Think ads, blog posts and podcasts aimed straight at your niche audience. For example, if you are slinging vegan baked goods, you would want to cozy up to people who are all about that healthy eating lifestyle.

Understand and integrate customer opinions

"Your most unhappy customers are your greatest source of learning."

- Bill Gates

Bill Gates hit the nail on the head with this quote. Customer feedback, whether positive or negative, is like gold for your business. It is your direct line to understanding what's working, what's not, and how you can improve. So, let's break down how to harness the power of customer feedback to take your business to the next level.

Listen up! Pay close attention to what your customers are saying, whether it is through surveys, reviews, or direct messages. Every comment, suggestion, and complaint is a nugget of insight waiting to be unearthed.

Once you have gathered feedback, it is time to analyze it like a detective on a mission. Look for common themes and trends. Are multiple customers pointing out the same issue? Or are there recurring compliments about a particular aspect of your business? Take note of these patterns, they will guide your next steps.

Now comes the fun part: taking action. Use the feedback you have gathered to make tangible improvements to your business. If customers are raving about your speedy delivery but griping about your website's clunky interface, focus your efforts on streamlining the user experience. And don't forget to keep your customers in the loop, let them know you have heard their feedback and are taking steps to address it.

But the feedback loop doesn't stop there. Keep the conversation going by circling back with your customers to see how they like the changes you have made. Are they singing your praises even louder? Or are there still areas that need tweaking? Use their responses to fine-tune your approach and keep improving.

Competitive Analysis

Competitive analysis is like peeking over the fence to see what your neighbors are up to. It is all about understanding what your competitors are doing right and where they are stumbling so you can stay ahead of the game. Here is a step-by-step guide to conducting a killer competitive analysis and learning from your competitor's successes and failures:

Identify Your Competitors: Start by making a list of your main competitors, those businesses that offer similar products or services to yours, and target the same audience. Don't just focus on direct competitors; consider indirect competitors and potential future rivals, too. Suppose you run a small coffee shop in a bustling downtown area. Your direct competitors might include other nearby coffee shops like "The Daily Grind" and "Bean & Brew," while indirect competitors could be fast-food chains offering coffee to-go, like Starbucks or Dunkin'.

Gather Information: Once you have got your list, it is time to do some sleuthing. Dive deep into your competitors' websites, social media profiles, marketing materials, and customer reviews to gather as much intel as possible. Pay attention to their products or services, pricing strategies, target audience, branding, marketing tactics, and customer feedback. Visit your competitors' websites, follow them on social media, and even visit their physical locations to gather intel. You might discover that "The Daily Grind" offers a loyalty program to reward repeat customers, while "Bean & Brew" emphasizes its commitment to fair-trade coffee beans on its website.

Analyze Strengths and Weaknesses: Now that you have got a treasure trove of data, it is time to roll up your sleeves and start analyzing. Identify your competitors' strengths. What are they doing really well? Maybe they have a killer product lineup, a strong brand presence, or top-notch customer service. On the flip side, pinpoint their weaknesses. Where are they falling short? Are their prices too high, their website outdated, or their customer service lacking? After digging into the data, you realize that "The Daily Grind" excels in creating a cozy atmosphere that keeps customers coming back, but their prices are slightly higher than average. Meanwhile, "Bean & Brew" has competitive pricing and a wide variety of coffee blends, but their website could use a facelift.

Learn from Successes: Take a closer look at your competitors' successes and figure out what you can learn from them. Are they killing it with a particular marketing campaign or product feature? Are they nailing their customer engagement strategy or dominating a specific niche? Borrow a page from their playbook and see how you can adapt their winning strategies to fit your own business. Taking a cue from "The Daily Grind," you decide to introduce a loyalty program at your own coffee shop to reward your most loyal customers. You also take note of "Bean & Brew's" extensive coffee menu and decide to expand your own offerings to attract more customers.

Learn from Failures: Equally important is learning from your competitors' failures. Take note of where they have stumbled, whether it is a botched product launch, a PR nightmare, or a customer service meltdown. Then, ask yourself: What went wrong? How could they have handled the situation better? And most importantly, how can you avoid making the same mistakes in your own business? You notice that "The Daily Grind" received negative reviews for slow service during peak hours. To avoid a similar fate, you invest in additional staff training and streamline your workflow to ensure quick and efficient service, even during busy times.

Identify Opportunities and Threats: Finally, use your competitive analysis to identify opportunities and threats in the market. Are there gaps in the market that your competitors are not addressing? Are there emerging trends or technologies that you could capitalize on? Conversely, are there threats on the horizon, like new competitors entering the scene or changing consumer preferences, that you need to be aware of and prepare for?

Staying relevant in a dynamic market

"Change is the law of life. And those who look only to the past or present are certain to miss the future."

- John F. Kennedy

In today's ever-evolving business landscape, adaptability is not just a nice-to-have. It is a must. Whether it is shifting consumer trends, technological advancements, or global crises like COVID-19, the ability to pivot and make adjustments on the fly can mean the difference between thriving and barely surviving.

Stay Up-to-Date: Keep your finger on the pulse of your industry by staying abreast of the latest trends and technologies. Whether it is attending industry conferences, subscribing to industry publications, or networking with other professionals, staying current ensures you are not caught off-guard by shifts in the market.

Engage with Your Customers: Your customers hold the key to your success, so it is crucial to listen to what they have to say. Engage with them online through social media, surveys, and feedback forms to understand their needs, desires, and pain points. By truly understanding your audience, you can tailor your products and services to better meet their needs.

Try New Things: Innovation drives progress, so don't be afraid to embrace new ideas and technologies. Be open to trying new strategies, products, and programs that have the potential to revolutionize your industry. Not every experiment will succeed, but by staying open-minded, you will position yourself to capitalize on emerging trends and stay ahead of the curve.

Make (Backup) Plans: As the saying goes, hope for the best but prepare for the worst. While you can't predict every twist and turn in the market, you can create contingency plans to weather potential storms. Whether it is mapping out best-case and worst-case scenarios or outlining strategies for different market conditions, having a plan in place ensures you are prepared for whatever the future holds.

Strengthen Your Brand: Your brand is more than just a logo or a tagline. It is the essence of your business. By cultivating a strong, unique, and memorable brand identity, you can differentiate yourself from competitors and build customer loyalty. But remember, a strong brand alone is not enough. You also need to be willing to adapt and evolve with the changing times.

The Importance of a Business Plan

Your business plan is like the roadmap to your entrepreneurial dreams. It lays out where you are headed, how you will get there, and what landmarks to watch out for along the way. But why is it so darn important, you ask? Well, think of it like this: would you set sail on a cross-country road trip without a GPS? Heck no! A business plan is your GPS for exploring the rocky terrain of entrepreneurship. It helps you define your goals, identify your target market, outline your strategies, and set a course for growth. Plus, it is your ticket to securing funding, attracting investors, and convincing potential partners that you mean business. So, trust me when I say that if you are serious about turning your business dreams into reality, a killer business plan is your first port of call. Now, let's talk turkey. Here is a simple template to get you started on crafting your own killer business plan:

- Executive Summary: Give them the elevator pitch, sum up your business, your goals and why you are going to crush it in one page or less.

- Company Description: Dive into the nitty-gritty of your business, what you do, who you serve, and why should they care?

- Market Analysis: Show them you have done your homework, who are your competitors, what's your target market, and where do you fit in?

- Organization and Management: Introduce the dream team, who's running the show, what's their expertise and how are you going to keep them in line?

- Products or Services: Lay it all out on the table: what are you selling, why is it awesome, and how are you going to make a buck?

- Marketing and Sales Strategy: Time to get creative. How are you going to spread the word, attract customers, and close those deals?

- Funding Request: Show them the money, how much do you need, what's it for, and what's in it for them?

- Financial Projections: Break out the crystal ball, what are your revenue projections expenses, and when are you going to start raking in the dough?

- Appendix: Dot your i's and, cross your t's, and toss in any extra goodies like resumes, contracts, or legal documents to seal the deal.

Identifying and preparing for potential business risks

Risk management is a critical aspect of business operations, encompassing strategies to identify, assess, and mitigate potential threats that could disrupt or harm a company's operations. Whether you are a startup or an established business, having robust risk management practices in place is essential for safeguarding your assets, reputation, and overall viability. Here is how to effectively manage risks in your business:

Identifying Risks:

Before you can manage risks, you need to identify them. Risks can come from various sources, including physical hazards, location-related factors, human behaviors, technological vulnerabilities, and strategic uncertainties. Conduct a comprehensive analysis of your business activities to identify potential risks that could impact your operations, finances, or reputation.

Assessing Risks:

Once you have identified potential risks, assess their likelihood and potential impact on your business. Prioritize risks based on their severity and probability of occurrence. Actuarial tables and statistical analysis can provide guidance in evaluating risks and determining appropriate risk management strategies.

Risk Management Strategies:

Implement risk management strategies to mitigate or eliminate identified risks. Common risk management techniques include:

- Acceptance: Some risks may be unavoidable or too costly to mitigate effectively. In such cases, accepting the risk and preparing contingency plans to minimize its impact can be the most practical approach.

- Transfer: Transfer the financial burden of certain risks to third parties through insurance policies or contractual agreements. For example, purchase insurance coverage for physical assets, liability risks or employee-related risks to mitigate financial losses.

- Reduction: Take proactive measures to reduce the likelihood or impact of identified risks. For instance, implement safety protocols, security measures, or disaster preparedness plans to minimize the risk of physical hazards or security breaches.

- Elimination: Eliminate or mitigate risks by implementing changes to your business processes, operations, or infrastructure. For example, replace outdated equipment, improve employee training programs, or diversify your supply chain to reduce dependence on a single supplier.

Insurance Coverage:

Insurance is a crucial tool for managing various types of risks. Consider purchasing insurance policies tailored to your specific business needs, such as property insurance, liability insurance, workers' compensation insurance, or cyber insurance. Regularly review your insurance coverage to ensure it aligns with your evolving risk profile and business activities.

Preventive Measures:

Prevention is often the most effective risk management strategy. Invest in employee training, conduct background checks, and enforce safety protocols to minimize the likelihood of accidents, fraud, or other human-related risks. Regular maintenance of physical premises, equipment, and IT systems can also help prevent potential hazards or disruptions.

Risk Management Oversight:

Assign responsibility for risk management to a designated individual or committee within your organization. Establish clear protocols for assessing, monitoring, and addressing risks on an ongoing basis. Regularly review and update your risk management policies and procedures to adapt to changing circumstances and emerging threats.

Plan Re-evaluation and Adaptation

In today's rapidly changing business landscape, adaptation is not just a luxury—it is a necessity for survival. The phrase "adapt or be left behind" serves as a stark reminder to business leaders that complacency is not an option. As industries evolve and opportunities emerge, companies must continuously evolve to stay relevant and competitive. Here are four key strategies to help your business adapt and thrive in an ever-changing environment:

Define a clear growth strategy:

To adapt effectively, you must have a clear understanding of where your business is headed and why. Define your growth strategy by identifying the problems you are solving and how you are uniquely positioned to solve them. Focus on sustainable growth that aligns with the needs of your customers and industry. For example, in the real estate industry, strategic growth may involve identifying market differentiators, prioritizing quality over quantity, and maintaining a personalized service experience for clients and agents alike.

Continually evolve and innovate:

Innovation is essential for staying ahead of the curve. Continuously seek ways to add value to your business proposition and address the evolving needs of your stakeholders. Don't wait for new technologies or tools to appear—actively seek or create them yourself. For instance, in the real estate industry, adapting to consumer preferences for a simpler, more convenient buying and selling experience may involve investing in tech-powered solutions like integrated CRM systems and predictive analytics to empower agents and enhance client satisfaction.

Always be a step ahead:

Anticipate industry trends and challenges to stay proactive rather than reactive. While you can't predict the future, you can prepare for potential disruptions and adapt quickly when necessary. For example, the shift towards mobile-driven home shopping prompted real estate companies to embrace digital platforms and social media early on. Being prepared for unexpected events, such as the pandemic-induced shutdowns, allows businesses to pivot swiftly and maintain momentum in the face of adversity.

Stay true to your founding mission:

As you adapt and grow, never lose sight of the core values and mission that inspired your business in the first place. Stay true to your founding principles of disruption, problem-solving, and innovation. Ensure that every decision aligns with your company culture and commitment to serving your community. For example, a company built on a culture of collaboration and partnership should prioritize these values even as it expands globally or undergoes acquisitions.

Chapter 10

Branding and Marketing Strategies

"Your brand is what other people say about you when you are not in the room."

-Founder of Virgin Group, Richard Branson

That is the essence of the importance of branding in today's competitive business landscape. Your brand is not just a logo or a slogan—it is the perception and reputation of your business in the minds of consumers. In a crowded marketplace, it is essential to give your business a distinct identity and make your brand stand out to attract customers. A strong brand not only differentiates you from your competitors but also builds trust, loyalty, and credibility with your target audience. By crafting a compelling brand story, delivering exceptional experiences, and consistently communicating your values and unique selling propositions, you can create a powerful connection with customers and drive long-term success for your business.

Developing a Unique Brand: Creating a brand that stands out

In today's fiercely competitive market, establishing a distinctive brand identity is paramount to capturing the attention of customers amidst a sea of competitors. With myriad businesses vying for consumer attention, it is imperative to craft a brand identity that not only sets you apart but also resonates deeply with your target audience. Here are some effective strategies to help you create a unique brand identity that stands out from the crowd:

Conduct Market Research: Start by conducting thorough market research to understand your target audience's demographics, preferences, and behaviors. This knowledge will inform your brand identity and help you tailor it to meet the specific needs and desires of your audience.

Define Your Brand's Purpose and Values: Clearly define your brand's purpose and values to give it a sense of direction and meaning. By articulating what your brand stands for and believes in, you can create a brand identity that authentically connects with your audience and sets you apart from competitors.

Develop a Unique Brand Voice: Your brand's voice is its personality—define it in terms of traits that resonate with your audience. Whether playful or serious, quirky or traditional, consistency is key across all communication channels to reinforce your brand's identity.

Tell a Compelling Brand Story: Craft a compelling narrative that communicates your brand's values, mission, and unique selling proposition. Your story should be authentic, emotionally resonant, and relatable to your target audience, helping to differentiate your business and forge a deeper connection with customers.

Create a Strong Visual Identity: Design a visually compelling brand identity encompassing your logo, color scheme, typography, and other visual elements. Consistency is crucial here, ensuring a cohesive and recognizable brand presence across all touchpoints.

Create Compelling Content: Produce high-quality, engaging content that positions your brand as a thought leader in your industry. This content should reflect your brand's values and resonate with your audience, fostering loyalty and trust over time.

Emphasize Customer Experience: Provide exceptional customer experiences at every touchpoint, from initial contact to post-purchase support. Personalization, responsiveness, and a focus on meeting customer needs are essential for building brand loyalty and standing out from competitors.

Emphasize Your Unique Selling Proposition: Identify and emphasize your unique selling proposition—the distinctive feature or benefit that sets your brand apart from competitors. Ensure consistency in highlighting your USP across all marketing channels to reinforce your brand's identity and value proposition.

Effective Marketing Techniques

In the ever-evolving landscape of business, effective marketing techniques are essential for reaching and engaging your audience amidst fierce competition. Marketing is the conduit through which ideas, products, or services are brought to the forefront of consumer consciousness. It revolves around understanding and fulfilling customer wants and needs to attract them to your business. Here are some strategies to craft a successful marketing approach:

Building a Marketing Strategy:

To effectively reach customers and build your brand, a well-defined marketing strategy is crucial. Setting clear goals aligned with your company's values and target audience is essential. Utilizing SMART goals—Specific, Measurable, Actionable, Relevant, and Time-bound— helps articulate and achieve these objectives. For instance, a coffee company aiming to launch a new flavor during the holidays may set a SMART goal to gain 1,000 new customers by the year's end.

Marketing Strategy vs. Marketing Plan:

While a marketing plan summarizes the company's objectives, the marketing strategy delineates the actionable components to achieve those goals. Strategies encompass various mediums and tactics to connect with potential customers and convert them into patrons. They typically have longer lifespans and include value propositions and brand dynamics. These strategies inform the marketing plan, detailing specific timelines and logistics for implementing marketing campaigns.

Marketing Strategies to Attract and Retain Customers:

Numerous marketing strategies can help businesses expand their customer base, encourage repeat business, and foster brand loyalty. Here are ten common techniques:

- Leverage social media: Engage with customers, share content, and build brand loyalty through social media platforms.

- Start a Blog: Provide valuable content to educate and inform customers, building authority and trust.

- Maximize Search Engine Optimization (SEO): Improve visibility in search engine results through strategic keyword optimization and engaging content.

- Create a Call to Action (CTA): Prompt customers to take action, such as making a purchase or signing up for a newsletter, through compelling CTAs.

- Engage Influencers: Partner with influencers to promote products or services to their dedicated audience.

- Build a Mailing List: Use email marketing to nurture leads, share promotions, and provide valuable content to subscribers.

- Create an Affiliate Program: Encourage customers to promote your products or services in exchange for incentives or commissions.

- Engage Customers with Chat: Provide real-time assistance and support through chat features on your website.

- Host Webinars: Educate and engage customers through interactive online seminars.

- Develop Customer Personas: Create detailed profiles of your ideal customers to personalize marketing efforts and tailor messaging to their needs and preferences.

Leveraging Social Media

Did you catch wind of the fact that a whopping 97 percent of potential buyers nowadays scout for brand info online before sealing the deal? It is a digital jungle out there, and having a solid online presence is your ticket to snagging a piece of that online market pie. By making yourself easy to find, offering up what you are all about, and forging connections with prospective customers, you are laying the groundwork for success in the digital realm.

Your digital presence is the virtual reflection of your brand out there on the web. It is the culmination of all your efforts to bridge the gap between you and your online audience. From slick websites to savvy social media, engaging blogs to targeted ads, it is all about making a splash in the digital pool. Building a robust digital presence takes time, effort, and some savvy strategies, but when done right, the rewards are sweet—think heightened brand visibility and a surge in conversions. So, how do you make your mark in the bustling online landscape? Here are a few pointers to get you started:

Serve Up Valuable Content: The content you churn out online is your brand's voice—the megaphone through which potential customers hear your message. It is all about keeping it simple, clear, and, above all, valuable. From eye-catching images to attention-grabbing posts, make sure your content speaks volumes about what you bring to the table.

Get a Handle on SEO: Want to boost your brand's visibility? SEO's your ticket. It is all about climbing the search engine ranks and getting your content seen by as many eyeballs as possible. From sprinkling in the right keywords to optimizing your site for mobile, a little SEO know-how goes a long way in getting your brand noticed.

Spruce Up Your Website: Your website is like your brand's digital storefront—it has got to be inviting, engaging, and, above all, conversion-friendly. From responsive design to killer CTAs, make sure your site's firing on all cylinders to turn those clicks into conversions.

Get Social: In today's digital age, being everywhere your customers are is key. Whether it is Facebook, Twitter, or Instagram, make sure your brand's got a presence on all the major platforms. The more touchpoints you have, the easier it is for customers to find you and connect with your brand.

Team Up: Success in the digital realm is a team sport. Get your teams working together to achieve your business goals and watch the magic happen. Whether it is brainstorming ideas or divvying up tasks, a little teamwork goes a long way in getting results.

Stay on Brand: Consistency is king when it comes to building a strong digital presence. From your logo to your brand voice, make sure everything's on point and in line with your brand's personality. It is all about creating a cohesive experience that keeps customers coming back for more.

Measure Up: Last but not least, make sure you are keeping tabs on how your digital efforts are performing. From tracking website traffic to monitoring social media engagement, analytics are your best friend when it comes to fine-tuning your digital strategy and driving results.

Building Customer Loyalty

"The key to success is to focus on the customer as the heart of your business."

- Anne M. Mulcahy.

In today's competitive marketplace, cultivating a loyal customer base is not just a luxury but a necessity for sustainable growth and long-term success. Loyal customers are not only repeat buyers, but they also serve as brand ambassadors, spreading positive word-of-mouth and driving new business through referrals. By prioritizing customer satisfaction, delivering exceptional service, and building meaningful relationships, businesses can earn the trust and loyalty of their customers, creating a solid foundation for continued success. From personalized experiences to loyalty programs and ongoing engagement, investing in customer loyalty is essential for businesses looking to thrive in an increasingly crowded and competitive landscape.

Before you can expect customers to be loyal to your brand, they need to know what you stand for. Take the time to define your brand's values, purpose, and unique selling points. Sit down with your team and brainstorm what sets your brand apart from the competition. Whether it is a commitment to sustainability, a dedication to quality craftsmanship, or a focus on customer empowerment, make sure these values are communicated clearly and authentically across all your marketing channels.

Knock their socks off with exceptional customer service:

Exceptional customer service is the cornerstone of building loyalty. From the moment a customer lands on your website to the interactions they have with your support team, every touchpoint should be designed to delight. Respond promptly to inquiries, resolve issues quickly and efficiently, and go above and beyond to exceed expectations. Remember, a happy customer is a loyal customer, so invest in training your team to deliver top-notch service at every opportunity.

Rally your biggest fans to spread the word:

Your most loyal customers can be your best brand advocates. These are the people who rave about your products or services on social media, recommend you to their friends and family, and leave glowing reviews online. Identify these brand evangelists and nurture these relationships. Engage with them on social media, offer them exclusive perks or discounts, and encourage them to share their experiences with others. By harnessing the power of word-of-mouth marketing, you can amplify your brand's reach and credibility.

Show them some love with a sweet loyalty program:

Everyone loves to feel appreciated, and a loyalty program is a great way to reward your most loyal customers for their continued support. Whether it is through points-based rewards, exclusive discounts, or special perks, incentivize repeat purchases and engagement. Not only does this show customers that you value their business, but it also encourages them to keep coming back for more.

Dig deeper to make a real connection:

Building customer loyalty is not just about transactions; it is about forging meaningful relationships. Take the time to get to know your customers on a personal level. Use data and analytics to understand their preferences, behavior, and needs. Tailor your communication and offerings to cater to their individual interests and pain points. By demonstrating that you understand and care about their unique needs, you can strengthen the bond between your brand and your customers.

Pick their brains for feedback:

Feedback is a valuable tool for improving your products, services, and overall customer experience. Actively solicit feedback from your customers through surveys, reviews, and social media channels. Pay attention to both positive and negative feedback and use it to identify areas for improvement. By involving customers in the feedback process, you not only show them that you value their opinions but also demonstrate your commitment to continuous improvement.

Always be striving to do better:

Building customer loyalty is an ongoing process that requires constant attention and effort. Stay agile and adaptable, and be willing to evolve with your customers' changing needs and expectations. Keep an eye on industry trends, competitor activity, and emerging technologies, and be proactive in adapting your strategies accordingly. By staying ahead of the curve and consistently delivering value to your customers, you can build a loyal customer base that will support your brand for years to come.

Chapter 11
Work-Life Balance in Entrepreneurship

"Your work is going to fill a large part of your life, and the only way to be truly satisfied is to do what you believe is great work. And the only way to do great work is to love what you do."

- Steve Jobs

These words ring especially true in the realm of entrepreneurship, where passion often fuels the pursuit of greatness. Yet, amidst the exhilarating journey of building something from the ground up, it is easy to lose sight of the importance of balance. In the chaotic dance between meetings, emails, and late-night brainstorming sessions, remember this: your well-being is just as vital as your business's success. Use the art of delegation, prioritize self-care, and cultivate boundaries that protect your time and energy. Strive not just for success but for a harmonious integration of work and life that nourishes both your professional ambitions and personal fulfillment. After all, the true measure of achievement lies not only in what you build but also in the joy you find along the way.

Setting Boundaries: Separating personal and professional life

In the dynamic landscape of entrepreneurship, the line between personal and professional life often blurs, leaving many individuals feeling overwhelmed and burnt out. However, mastering the art of setting boundaries can be the key to reclaiming control and achieving a healthier work-life balance. In this discussion, we will explore various strategies for establishing clear boundaries that allow entrepreneurs to thrive in both their personal and professional endeavors.

Saying No: The Power Move

Learning to say no is a skill that every entrepreneur must master. While the desire to please clients, investors and colleagues is understandable, it is essential to recognize when taking on additional commitments will stretch you too thin. Saying no is not a sign of weakness – it is a powerful assertion of your priorities and limitations. By setting boundaries around what you are willing to take on, you can safeguard your time and energy for the tasks that truly matter, ultimately enhancing your productivity and well-being.

Setting Work Hours: Clocking In and Clocking Out

In today's digital age, the concept of traditional work hours has become increasingly blurred. Many entrepreneurs find themselves working around the clock, responding to emails at all hours, and sacrificing their personal time in the process. However, setting clear work hours is essential for maintaining a healthy work-life balance. Whether you adhere to a strict 9-to-5 schedule or prefer a more flexible approach, establishing boundaries around when you are "on the clock" allows you to compartmentalize your professional responsibilities and carve out dedicated time for rest and rejuvenation.

Prioritizing Personal Time: Making Room for Joy

Amidst the demands of entrepreneurship, it is easy to neglect personal time and the activities that bring us joy outside of work. However, prioritizing personal time is essential for maintaining overall well-being and preventing burnout. From spending quality time with loved ones and pursuing hobbies and interests to simply taking a moment to relax and unwind, carving out space for these activities is non-negotiable. By intentionally prioritizing personal time, entrepreneurs can recharge their batteries, gain fresh perspectives, and ultimately become more effective in their professional pursuits.

Efficiently managing your time for maximum productivity

Time management is the cornerstone of success for any entrepreneur. Effectively managing your time allows you to prioritize tasks, minimize distractions, and maximize productivity. Here, we will delve into some key strategies for mastering time management and achieving a harmonious balance between life and work as an entrepreneur.

Set Clear Goals and Priorities

Begin by establishing clear goals for both your professional and personal life. Break these goals down into smaller, actionable tasks and prioritize them based on their importance and urgency. By focusing your time and energy on tasks that align with your overarching objectives, you can ensure that you are making progress toward your goals every day.

Plan and Organize Your Schedule

Create a daily or weekly schedule that outlines your commitments, deadlines, and priorities. Use tools such as calendars, planners, or digital apps to keep track of your schedule and stay organized. Allocate specific blocks of time for different tasks, making sure to include buffer periods for unforeseen circumstances or breaks to rest and recharge.

Utilize Time Blocking

Time blocking involves dedicating specific time periods to focus on particular tasks or types of work. By grouping similar tasks together and allocating uninterrupted blocks of time to tackle them, you can enhance your focus and productivity. Whether you are responding to emails, working on creative projects, or conducting meetings, designate specific time slots for each activity to minimize distractions and optimize efficiency.

Delegate and Outsource

Recognize that you can't do everything yourself and be willing to delegate tasks or outsource certain responsibilities when necessary. Identify tasks that can be effectively handled by others, whether you are hiring employees, collaborating with freelancers, or utilizing automation tools. Delegating allows you to free up valuable time for high-priority tasks and strategic decision-making, ultimately increasing your overall productivity.

Practice Time Management Techniques

Explore various time management techniques to find what works best for you. Techniques such as the Pomodoro Technique or the Eisenhower Matrix can be valuable tools for boosting productivity. Experiment with different methods to discover which ones align with your working style and preferences.

1. Pomodoro Technique:

The Pomodoro Technique is a time management method developed by Francesco Cirillo in the late 1980s. It involves breaking your work into intervals, traditionally 25 minutes in length, separated by short breaks. Here is how it typically works:

- Choose a task you want to work on.

- Set a timer for 25 minutes (one "Pomodoro").

- Work on the task with full focus until the timer rings.

- Take a short break (usually 5 minutes).

Repeat the process, taking a longer break (around 15-30 minutes) after every fourth Pomodoro.

The Pomodoro Technique helps improve focus and productivity by breaking work into manageable chunks and providing regular breaks to rest and recharge. It can be particularly effective for tasks that require concentration and creative thinking.

2. Eisenhower Matrix:

The Eisenhower Matrix, also known as the Urgent-Important Matrix, is a decision-making framework attributed to former U.S. President Dwight D. Eisenhower. It categorizes tasks into four quadrants based on their urgency and importance:

- Quadrant 1: Urgent and Important (Do First) – Tasks that require immediate attention and have significant consequences if not addressed promptly.

- Quadrant 2: Important but Not Urgent (Schedule) – Tasks that contribute to long-term goals and require proactive planning and prioritization.

- Quadrant 3: Urgent but Not Important (Delegate) – Tasks that demand immediate action but don't contribute significantly to your goals. These tasks can often be delegated to others.

- Quadrant 4: Not Urgent and Not Important (Eliminate) – Tasks that are neither urgent nor important and can be eliminated or postponed without consequences.

The Eisenhower Matrix helps individuals identify and prioritize tasks based on their significance and deadline, allowing them to focus their time and energy on activities that align with their goals and values. By categorizing tasks into these quadrants, individuals can make more informed decisions about where to allocate their resources effectively.

Both the Pomodoro Technique and the Eisenhower Matrix are powerful tools for managing time and increasing productivity, but their effectiveness may vary depending on individual preferences and work styles.

Limit Distractions and Stay Focused

Identify common distractions in your work environment and take steps to minimize them. This might involve turning off notifications, setting boundaries with colleagues or family members, or creating a designated workspace free from distractions. Additionally, practice mindfulness techniques such as deep breathing or meditation to improve your ability to stay focused and present in the moment.

Regularly evaluate your time management strategies and make adjustments as needed. Reflect on what's working well and where you could improve, and be open to trying new approaches. Flexibility and adaptability are key qualities of successful entrepreneurs, so don't be afraid to tweak your methods until you find the perfect formula for maximizing your productivity and achieving a healthy work-life balance.

Dealing with Burnout

Exploring the turbulent waters of entrepreneurial life can sometimes feel like a high-stakes game of endurance. But here is the kicker: burnout doesn't discriminate. So, let's dial it down a notch and chat about how to sidestep that burnout trap.

Spot the Burnout:

- Feeling Like a Zombie: Ever feel like you are running on empty, even after catching some Z's? That's your body's way of saying, "Hey, slow down!"

- Motivation? What's That? If your get-up-and-go got up and went, leaving you feeling like a productivity zombie, it might be time to reassess your workload.

- Grumpy Pants: Irritability and negativity creeping in? That's not just a case of the Mondays – it could be burnout knocking at your door.

- Checking Out: When you start mentally clocking out of your own business, it is a clear sign that burnout has taken the wheel.

- Physical Red Flags: Headaches, muscle tension, and stomach knots – oh my! Your body's giving you a not-so-subtle nudge to pump the brakes.

Keep Burnout at Bay:

- Get Real: Set realistic goals, and don't bite off more than you can chew. It is okay to say no – your sanity will thank you.

- Draw the Line: Work-life balance is not just a buzzword – it is a lifeline. Schedule downtime and stick to it like your business depends on it (spoiler alert: it does).

- Pass the Baton: You are not a one-person show. Delegate tasks, outsource, and give yourself some breathing room.

- Chill Out: Stress management is not just about downing chamomile tea. Embrace mindfulness, get moving, or find whatever floats your relaxation boat.

- Lean on Your Crew: Friends, family, fellow entrepreneurs – they are your support squad. Don't be afraid to reach out when the going gets tough.

Tackle Burnout Head-On:

- Hit Pause: Burnout got you down? Take a breather. Disconnect, unwind, and do whatever it takes to refill your tank.

- Reality Check: Take a good, hard look at your goals and priorities. It might be time to pivot or readjust your course.

So, there you have it – a no-nonsense guide to dodging burnout in the wild world of entrepreneurship. Remember, it is not about sprinting to the finish line – it is about pacing yourself for the marathon ahead. So, kick back, take a breather, and keep on hustling – burnout doesn't stand a chance against your resilience.

The Role of Support Systems

Being an entrepreneur is not a solo journey – it is a team sport. And when the going gets tough, having a solid support system in place can make all the difference. Let's face it – entrepreneurship is a rollercoaster ride of highs and lows. In those moments when self-doubt creeps in or setbacks threaten to derail your progress, having a support system to lean on can provide the emotional resilience you need to keep pushing forward. Knowing you are not alone in the trenches can bolster your spirits and help you weather the storm.

When you are knee-deep in the day-to-day grind of running a business, it is easy to lose sight of the bigger picture. That's where your support network comes in. Family members, friends, and fellow entrepreneurs can offer fresh perspectives and valuable insights that help you see challenges from new angles and identify potential solutions.

Talking to someone you trust or seeking advice from a mentor can help you make hard decisions with confidence.

Entrepreneurship is notorious for blurring the lines between work and personal life. But having a strong support system in place can help you maintain a healthy balance between the two. Family and friends can provide much-needed encouragement to step away from work and prioritize self-care, while networks and communities can offer opportunities for social connection and rejuvenation outside of the business realm. By nurturing relationships with your support system, you can ensure that your entrepreneurial journey doesn't come at the expense of your well-being and relationships.

Your support system is not just there to offer moral support – it can also open doors to new opportunities and connections. Your network can help you in many ways, like introducing you to potential clients or investors, sharing useful resources and contacts, or working together on projects and ideas. It's like a springboard that can boost your growth and expansion. By nurturing relationships within your support system and actively engaging with your broader network, you can amplify your reach and tap into a wealth of opportunities that propel your business forward.

In essence, the role of support systems in entrepreneurship goes far beyond mere encouragement – it is about finding strength, perspective, and opportunities in the company of those who believe in your vision and champion your success. So don't go it alone – lean on your tribe, celebrate the wins together, and navigate the challenges as a united front.

After all, behind every successful entrepreneur is a rock-solid support system cheering them on every step of the way.

Chapter 12

Innovation and Creativity in Business

"Innovation distinguishes between a leader and a follower,"

Steve Jobs once famously declared. And truer words were never spoken. Let's talk about innovation and creativity in business – the secret sauce that sets the trailblazers apart from the crowd. See, in today's fast-paced world, standing still is akin to moving backward. It is not just about doing things differently; it is about doing things better, smarter, and more creatively. Innovation is not reserved for the big shots with fancy titles – it is a mindset, a way of approaching challenges with a fresh perspective and a willingness to think outside the box. So, whether you are a startup founder, a seasoned entrepreneur, or just dreaming up your next big idea, remember this: innovation is not a luxury – it is a necessity. Embrace the unknown, chase those wild ideas, and dare to disrupt the status quo. After all, the future belongs to those who dare to innovate.

Fostering Creativity

The lifeblood of any successful business. Creating an environment where new ideas flourish is not just about having a ping-pong table in the breakroom (although that can help!). It is about fostering a culture that celebrates creativity and encourages out-of-the-box thinking at every turn. Here are some strategies to help you cultivate a fertile ground for innovation:

Encourage Open Communication:

First things first – create an atmosphere where everyone feels comfortable sharing their ideas, no matter how wild or unconventional. Foster open communication channels where team members can freely brainstorm, collaborate, and bounce ideas off each other without fear of judgment. Remember, great ideas can come from anyone, so make sure everyone has a seat at the table.

Cherish the Diversity:

Diversity is not just a buzzword – it is a catalyst for creativity. Surround yourself with people from diverse backgrounds, perspectives, and skill sets. Embracing diversity enriches your team with a variety of viewpoints and experiences, sparking new ideas and challenging the status quo. Celebrate differences and create opportunities for collaboration across departments and disciplines.

Provide Resources and Support:

Give your team the tools they need to turn their ideas into reality. Demonstrate your commitment to your team's success by offering access to the latest technology, investing in their professional growth, and providing financial backing for creative projects. A little support can go a long way in fueling creativity and innovation.

Foster a Culture of Experimentation:

Encourage experimentation and risk-taking within your organization. Create a safe space where failure is viewed as a natural part of the creative process rather than a reason to retreat. Encourage your team to test out new ideas, learn from their mistakes, and iterate until they find success. Remember, some of the greatest innovations come from taking calculated risks.

Lead by Example:

As a leader, your actions speak louder than words. Lead by example and demonstrate your own willingness to accept creativity and innovation. Show your team that you are not afraid to think outside the box, take risks, and pursue ambitious goals. Your enthusiasm and passion for innovation will inspire others to do the same.

Recognize and Reward Creativity:

Finally, don't forget to recognize and reward creativity within your organization. Show appreciation for individuals who bring innovative ideas to the table, whether it's through formal recognition programs, monetary rewards, or a simple heartfelt thank-you. By celebrating creativity, you reinforce its value and encourage others to follow suit.

Embracing Innovation

In today's rapidly evolving landscape, it is not enough to simply keep pace – you have to lead the pack with fresh ideas and forward-thinking strategies. But fear not, fellow entrepreneurs, because I have got a few tricks up my sleeve to help you accept innovation and keep your business on the cutting edge:

Foster Curiosity:

Feed your curiosity like it is fuel for the fire. Stay hungry for knowledge, trends, and emerging technologies in your industry. Stay open to new opportunities by immersing yourself in industry blogs, participating in workshops, and connecting with insiders in your field. The more you know, the more inspiration you will find for innovative solutions.

Customer-Centric Innovation:

Listen closely to the heartbeat of your business – your customers. Pay attention to their needs, desires, and pain points, and let their feedback guide your innovation efforts. Prioritize understanding your customers' needs and preferences, whether it's through surveys, focus groups, or individual conversations. Then, use that insight to craft innovative products or services that exceed their expectations.

Cultivate a Culture of Creativity:

Plant the seeds of innovation within your team by fostering a culture of creativity and collaboration. Encourage brainstorming sessions, idea swaps, and out-of-the-box thinking. Create an environment where every team member feels empowered to contribute their unique perspective and experiment with new ideas. Remember, innovation thrives in an atmosphere of openness and exploration.

Accept Technology as Your Ally:

Technology is not just a tool – it is a catalyst for innovation. Keep your finger on the pulse of emerging technologies that have the potential to revolutionize your industry. Whether it is AI, IoT, or machine learning, explore how these technologies can be harnessed to drive innovation and create value for your customers.

Develop the Spirit of Experimentation:

Have a mindset of experimentation and iteration. Don't be afraid to test out new concepts, even if they seem unconventional or risky. Learn from your failures, pivot when necessary, and celebrate your successes along the way. Remember, innovation is a journey, not a destination – so keep experimenting, keep learning, and keep pushing the boundaries of what's possible.

Innovation thrives in environments that are agile and adaptable. Use agile methodologies and lean principles to streamline your innovation process and respond quickly to changing market dynamics. Stay nimble, stay flexible, and be ready to pivot on a dime when opportunity knocks.

Creative Blocks: Strategies to keep ideas flowing

Ever find yourself staring at a blank page or hitting a mental roadblock when you are trying to come up with your next big idea? Welcome to the world of creative blocks – a frustrating yet all-too-common challenge faced by entrepreneurs and creative minds alike. It is like hitting a wall, where no matter how hard you try, the ideas just won't flow. But fear not, my fellow trailblazers, because I have some tried-and-true strategies to help you smash through those creative barriers and keep the ideas flowing:

Take a Break:

Sometimes, the best way to overcome a creative block is to step away from the problem altogether. Take a walk, grab a cup of coffee, or engage in a completely unrelated activity to give your mind a chance to recharge. You will be amazed at how often inspiration strikes when you least expect it.

Change Your Environment:

Shake things up by changing your surroundings. Head to a coffee shop, park, or coworking space for a change of scenery. Sometimes, a new environment can stimulate fresh ideas and break you out of your creative rut.

Engage in Mindless Activities:

Give your brain a break by engaging in mindless activities like doodling, knitting, or coloring. These repetitive tasks can help quiet your mind and create space for new ideas to emerge.

Brainstorm with Others:

Two heads are better than one, as they say. Gather your team or a group of trusted friends and engage in a brainstorming session. Feed off each other's energy and bounce ideas around until something sparks.

Try a Different Approach:

If you have been approaching the problem from the same angle with no success, it might be time to try a different approach. Break the problem down into smaller pieces, flip it on its head, or tackle it from a completely different perspective.

Embrace Constraints:

Sometimes, constraints can actually fuel creativity. Welcome the constraints you encounter, such as tight budgets, deadlines, or limited resources, and leverage them as opportunities to develop innovative solutions.

Don't Be Afraid to Fail:

Lastly, don't let the fear of failure hold you back. Creativity thrives in an environment where experimentation is encouraged, and mistakes are seen as learning opportunities. Acknowledge the process, trust your instincts, and remember that some of the greatest innovations arise from taking calculated risks.

Expose yourself to new ideas and experiences to fuel your creativity. Read books, watch TED talks, attend workshops, or explore art galleries – whatever gets your creative juices flowing.

Merge innovative ideas with feasible business strategies

There is a tightrope between creativity and practicality – a balancing act that every entrepreneur knows all too well. On the one hand, you have got these wild, out-of-the-box ideas that make your heart race with excitement. On the other hand, you have got to keep your feet firmly planted on the ground and make sure those ideas actually make sense for your business. It is like trying to juggle fire and ice – tricky but not impossible. So, let me share some strategies to help you merge innovative ideas with feasible business strategies:

Start with Your Why:

Before diving headfirst into the realm of creativity, take a step back and revisit your why. What problem are you trying to solve? What value are you aiming to deliver to your customers? By anchoring your creative endeavors in a clear understanding of your purpose and goals, you will ensure that your innovative ideas are aligned with your overarching business objectives.

Conduct Market Research:

Creativity without context is like a ship without a compass – it might look impressive, but it is bound to veer off course. Before fully committing to an innovative idea, conduct thorough market research to validate its feasibility and potential demand. Understand your target audience, identify market trends, and assess the competitive landscape to ensure that your creative concept has legs to stand on.

Prototype and Test:

Don't wait until you have a fully fleshed-out product or service to test the waters – start small with prototypes or minimum viable products (MVPs) and gather feedback from real users. Use this iterative approach to refine your innovative ideas based on real-world insights and validate their practicality and market fit before scaling up.

Balance Risk and Reward:

Innovation inherently involves taking risks, but it is essential to strike a balance between ambition and prudence. Evaluate the potential risks and rewards associated with each innovative idea and weigh them against your risk tolerance and resource constraints. Aim for a calculated approach that maximizes upside potential while minimizing downside risk.

Collaborate and Iterate:

Two heads are better than one, as they say. Collaborate with diverse team members, mentors, or industry experts to brainstorm and refine your innovative ideas. Leverage their perspectives and expertise to identify blind spots, mitigate risks, and optimize your strategies for practical implementation. Use an iterative approach that allows for continuous improvement based on feedback and insights from stakeholders.

Remember, innovation doesn't have to be at odds with feasibility – with the right approach and mindset, you can turn your wildest ideas into tangible business successes.

Chapter 13
Navigating Legal and Ethical Challenges

"In the end, all business operations can be reduced to three words: people, product, and profits."

- Lee Iacocca.

Running a business is not just about chasing profits – it is about steering through a complex web of legal and ethical considerations that can make or break your success. From ensuring compliance with regulations to upholding moral standards, the journey of entrepreneurship is fraught with challenges on both fronts. From safeguarding customer data to exploring intellectual property rights or grappling with ethical dilemmas, staying on the right side of the law and maintaining integrity are non-negotiables. So, my fellow entrepreneurs, buckle up and get ready to tackle these legal and ethical hurdles head-on. Remember, in the game of business, playing by the rules is not just a suggestion – it is the only way to win in the long run.

Basic legal knowledge every entrepreneur should have.

Now, I know legal jargon might not be the most thrilling topic, but trust me when I say that understanding the basics of business law is absolutely essential for any entrepreneur. Think of it as your roadmap for exploring the often-murky waters of the business world. So why exactly do we need business laws? Well, picture this: you have got this brilliant business idea, you are ready to hit the ground running and then bam – you hit a legal snag that brings your dreams to a screeching halt.

Not exactly the plot twist you were hoping for, right? That's where business laws come in. They provide the framework for conducting business ethically, protecting your rights and assets, and ensuring a level playing field for all players in the game. So, let's roll up our sleeves and delve into some of the key areas of business law that every entrepreneur should have a handle on:

Entity Formation:

Choosing the right legal structure for your business. Each business entity—whether it's a sole proprietorship, partnership, corporation, or LLC—carries its own unique set of rights, responsibilities, and tax considerations. Do your homework, weigh the pros and cons, and select the structure that best suits your business goals and needs.

Contracts and Agreements:

Next up, let's talk contracts. These legal agreements govern everything from partnerships and employment relationships to vendor agreements and customer transactions. Make sure you understand the terms and conditions of any contract you enter into, and do not hesitate to seek legal advice if you are unsure about any aspect of the agreement.

Intellectual Property Rights:

Your intellectual property –your brand name, logo, inventions, or creative works – is your most valuable asset. Protect it like your business depends on it (spoiler alert: it does). Familiarize yourself with trademarks, copyrights, patents, and trade secrets, and take steps to safeguard your intellectual property from infringement or misappropriation.

Employment Law:

If you have got employees, you have got to play by the rules. Familiarize yourself with labor laws, anti-discrimination laws, wage and hour regulations, and workplace safety standards to ensure compliance and foster a fair and equitable work environment.

Taxation:

Taxes are the inevitable thorn in every entrepreneur's side. Understand your tax obligations, deductions, and filing requirements to avoid running afoul of the IRS. Consider consulting with a tax professional to ensure you are taking advantage of all available tax-saving strategies while staying on the right side of the law.

Regulatory Compliance:

Last but certainly not least regulatory compliance. Depending on your industry and location, you may be subject to a myriad of regulations governing everything from environmental protection and consumer safety to data privacy and advertising practices. Stay informed about relevant regulations and ensure your business operations are in compliance to avoid costly fines or legal penalties.

Balancing profit with ethical considerations.

Ethical decision-making boils down to making choices that are not only legal and financially sound but also morally defensible. It is about doing the right thing, even when no one is watching, and upholding principles of integrity, fairness, and respect for all stakeholders involved. Now, you might be wondering, how do we balance the pursuit of profit with ethical considerations? Well, let me break it down for you:

Define Your Values:

First things first – get clear on your values as a business owner. What principles are non-negotiables for you? Honesty, transparency, sustainability, or social responsibility? Identify the values that will serve as your guiding light in making ethical decisions.

Consider Stakeholder Impact:

Think beyond the bottom line and consider the impact of your decisions on all stakeholders involved – customers, employees, suppliers, investors, and the community at large. Ask yourself: Does this decision align with our values? Will it benefit or harm those affected by it? Taking a stakeholder-centric approach ensures that you are considering the broader implications of your actions.

Seek Input and Perspective:

Do not go it alone – seek input and perspective from others when faced with ethical dilemmas. Consult with trusted advisors, mentors, or members of your team to gain different viewpoints and insights. Sometimes, an outside perspective can shed light on blind spots or unintended consequences you may not have considered.

Conduct Ethical Impact Assessments:

Before making major decisions, conduct ethical impact assessments to evaluate the potential consequences of your actions. Consider the short-term and long-term implications on various stakeholders, as well as any ethical risks or conflicts that may arise. This proactive approach allows you to identify potential ethical pitfalls and mitigate them before they escalate.

Lead by Example:

As a leader, your actions speak louder than words. Lead by example and demonstrate your commitment to ethical decision-making through your own behavior and choices. Foster a culture of integrity and accountability within your organization, where ethical considerations are prioritized in every aspect of business operations.

Be Transparent and Accountable:

Transparency breeds trust – be open and honest about your decision-making process and the rationale behind your choices. Take ownership of your decisions and be willing to stand behind them, even if they are unpopular or difficult. By being transparent and accountable, you build credibility and goodwill with your stakeholders.

Continuously Learn and Improve:

Ethical decision-making is not a one-time event – it is an ongoing process of learning and improvement. Stay informed about emerging ethical issues and best practices in your industry, and be willing to adapt your approach as needed. Reflect on past decisions, learn from your mistakes, and strive to continuously raise the bar for ethical conduct within your organization.

Intellectual Property Rights

Intellectual property rights, simply put, are legal protections granted to individuals or organizations for their intellectual creations, such as inventions, artistic works, designs, and brand identities. These rights give you exclusive control over the use and distribution of your intellectual property, allowing you to prevent others from copying, using, or profiting from your creations without your permission. Now, you might be wondering, how do we go about protecting our ideas and products? Let's look into that!

Patents:

If you have a groundbreaking invention or innovation, consider filing for a patent to protect your intellectual property rights. A patent grants you exclusive rights to your invention for a specified period, typically 20 years, preventing others from making, using, or selling your invention without your consent. Be sure to conduct a thorough patent search to ensure your invention is unique and eligible for patent protection before filing your application.

Trademarks:

Your brand identity is your most valuable asset – protect it with a trademark. A trademark grants you exclusive rights to use your brand name, logo, or slogan in connection with your products or services, distinguishing them from those of others. Registering your trademark with the appropriate government agency provides you with legal recourse against unauthorized use or infringement by competitors.

Copyrights:

If you are a creative soul –an artist, writer, musician, or filmmaker – copyrights are your best friend. A copyright grants you exclusive rights to reproduce, distribute, and publicly display your original works of authorship, such as books, music, films, and artwork. Registering your copyrights with the copyright office provides you with additional legal protections and remedies in case of infringement.

Trade Secrets:

Some things are best kept under lock and key – that's where trade secrets come in. Trade secrets are confidential information that gives your business a competitive edge, such as formulas, processes, customer lists, or marketing strategies. Protect your trade secrets by implementing strict confidentiality measures and non-disclosure agreements with employees, partners, and vendors.

Contracts and Non-Disclosure Agreements (NDAs):

When sharing confidential information with third parties, such as employees, contractors, or business partners, be sure to use contracts and non-disclosure agreements (NDAs) to safeguard your intellectual property rights. These legal agreements outline the terms and conditions of the relationship, including obligations to maintain confidentiality and restrictions on the use of proprietary information.

Monitor and Enforce Your Rights:

Protecting your intellectual property does not end with obtaining legal protections – you have to be proactive in monitoring and enforcing your rights. Keep an eye out for unauthorized use or infringement of your intellectual property and take swift action to address any violations. This may involve sending cease and desist letters, filing infringement lawsuits, or pursuing other legal remedies to protect your rights and preserve the value of your intellectual property assets.

Dealing with red tape and regulatory challenges.

Red tape and bureaucratic hurdles are the thorns on the side of every entrepreneur. Picture this: you have got this brilliant business idea, you are raring to go, and then bam – you hit a wall of paperwork, regulations, and endless hoops to jump through. It is enough to make even the most seasoned entrepreneur want to throw in the towel. But fear not, my fellow trailblazers, because I have some strategies to help you navigate the labyrinth of bureaucracy and deal with regulatory challenges like a pro:

Understand the Landscape:

First things first – get to know the lay of the land. Research and familiarize yourself with the regulatory requirements and compliance obligations relevant to your industry and location. Whether it is zoning laws, licensing requirements, or tax regulations, ignorance is not bliss when it comes to red tape. The more you know, the better equipped you will be to navigate the bureaucratic maze.

Build Relationships:

Next up, build relationships with key stakeholders who can help smooth the path ahead. Whether it is government officials, industry associations, or legal advisors, cultivate connections with individuals who have the knowledge and influence to guide you through regulatory challenges. Do not be afraid to ask for help or seek advice from those who have navigated similar waters before.

Stay Organized:

Organization is your best friend when it comes to dealing with red tape. Keep meticulous records of all documentation, correspondence, and compliance efforts related to your business. Create a centralized system for managing regulatory requirements, deadlines, and renewal dates to ensure nothing slips through the cracks. By staying organized, you will be better prepared to address regulatory challenges efficiently and effectively.

Go for Professional Assistance:

When in doubt, enlist the help of professionals who specialize in regulating challenges. Investing in expert assistance, whether it's hiring a lawyer, accountant, or regulatory consultant, can ultimately save you time, money, and headaches down the road. These professionals can provide valuable guidance, advice, and support to help you navigate complex regulatory landscapes with confidence.

Advocate for Change:

Do not be afraid to speak up and advocate for changes to outdated or burdensome regulations that stifle innovation and entrepreneurship. Join industry associations, participate in advocacy campaigns, and engage with policymakers to voice your concerns and propose solutions. By working together with other entrepreneurs and stakeholders, you can drive meaningful change and create a more conducive regulatory environment for businesses like yours.

Stay Flexible and Persistent:

Finally, remember that dealing with red tape is often a marathon, not a sprint. Stay flexible, adaptable, and persistent in your efforts to overcome regulatory challenges. Keep your eye on the prize – building a successful business – and do not let bureaucratic hurdles derail your dreams. With patience, perseverance, and a strategic approach, you can conquer red tape and emerge victorious on the other side.

Chapter 14

The Role of Technology in Modern Business

"As we look ahead into the next century, leaders will be those who empower others."

- Bill Gates.

From artificial intelligence and big data analytics to cloud computing and blockchain technology, the arsenal of tools at our disposal in this age is nothing short of mind-boggling. Technology is not just a means to an end – it is the fuel that powers innovation, transforms industries, and propels businesses into the future. So, whether you are a startup founder, a seasoned entrepreneur, or just dipping your toes into the entrepreneurial waters, remember this: Use technology, harness its power, and you will unlock a world of endless opportunities to empower yourself and others on the path to success.

Leveraging Tech for Efficiency: Using technology to streamline operations.

In today's fast-paced world, time is money, and efficiency is the name of the game. Fortunately, we live in an era where technology offers a treasure trove of tools and solutions to help us work smarter, not harder. So, how can you harness the power of tech to streamline your operations and boost your productivity as an entrepreneur?

Identify Pain Points:

First things first – take a good, hard look at your business operations and identify areas where you are spending too much time, money, or effort. Identifying your pain points, from manual data entry to repetitive tasks or communication bottlenecks, is the initial step in discovering technological solutions to alleviate them.

Invest in the Right Tools:

Once you have identified your pain points, it is time to invest in the right tools to streamline your operations. Whether it is project management software, customer relationship management (CRM) systems, accounting software, or collaboration platforms, there is a wealth of tech solutions out there designed to make your life easier. Do your research, test out different options, and invest in tools that align with your business needs and budget.

Automate Repetitive Tasks:

Say goodbye to tedious, repetitive tasks that eat up your time and energy. Leverage automation tools to handle routine processes such as email marketing, data entry, invoicing, and social media posting. By automating these tasks, you free up valuable time to focus on more high-value activities that drive growth and innovation in your business.

Use Cloud Computing:

Take your business to the cloud and enjoy the benefits of anytime, anywhere access to your data and applications. Cloud computing offers scalability, flexibility, and cost-effectiveness, allowing you to scale your operations up or down as needed without the hassle of managing physical servers.

Streamline Communication:

Communication is key to any successful business, but it can also be a major productivity drain if not managed effectively. Invest in communication tools such as instant messaging platforms, video conferencing software, and project management apps to streamline collaboration and keep your team connected.

Technology is constantly evolving, so it is important to continuously evaluate and improve your tech stack to stay ahead of the curve. Keep an eye out for new tools, features, and updates that can further enhance efficiency and productivity in your business. Solicit feedback from your team, monitor key performance indicators, and be willing to adapt and iterate based on what's working and what's not.

E-commerce and Online Presence

In today's digital era, carving out a space for your business in the vast online landscape is not just advantageous – it is essential for long-term success. So, how exactly can you go about crafting a robust online presence that sets you apart from the competition? Let's discover!

Craft an Engaging Website:

Your website serves as the digital storefront for your business, so it is crucial to make a stellar first impression. Invest in professional web design that not only looks visually appealing but also offers seamless navigation and a user-friendly experience. Ensure that your website is optimized for mobile devices, as an increasing number of users access the web from smartphones and tablets.

Master the Art of SEO:

Search engine optimization (SEO) is the cornerstone of a successful online presence. Conduct thorough keyword research to identify the terms and phrases your target audience is searching for and strategically incorporate them into your website content, meta tags, and URLs. Regularly update your content and earn backlinks from reputable sources to improve your search engine rankings and drive organic traffic to your site.

Engage with Your Audience on Social Media:

Social media platforms offer invaluable opportunities to connect with your audience, build relationships, and promote your brand. Identify the platforms where your target demographic is most active and create compelling content that resonates with them. Discover imaginative ways to interact with your audience and nurture a sense of community by offering behind-the-scenes insights into your business, hosting live Q&A sessions, or organizing interactive contests.

Harness the Power of E-Commerce Platforms:

If you are in the business of selling products online, e-commerce platforms are your best friend. Choose a platform that aligns with your business needs and offers the features and flexibility you require. Customize your storefront to reflect your brand identity, optimize your product listings for search visibility, and provide a seamless checkout experience to minimize cart abandonment and maximize conversions.

Prioritize Customer Service and Feedback:

In the digital realm, excellent customer service is paramount. Respond promptly to customer inquiries and feedback and go above and beyond to exceed their expectations. Leverage customer relationship management (CRM) tools to track interactions and personalize your communications. Solicit feedback from your customers through surveys, reviews, and social media polls and use this information to continuously improve your products, services, and overall customer experience.

Cybersecurity for Startups

Think of protecting your business from online threats, like building a fortress to keep out sneaky invaders. Just like you need a sturdy lock on your front door, you need strong passwords to keep cyber-criminals out of your digital spaces. Think of a password like your secret code to enter your castle – make it unique, long, and hard to guess.

Firewalls are like the guards standing watch at the walls of your castle. They keep an eye on who's trying to get in and block any suspicious characters trying to sneak past. Your employees are the knights who defend your castle from cyber-attacks. Make sure they know how to recognize the tricks and traps set by cyber-criminals. Teach them to be cautious of suspicious emails or links – it is like giving them a crash course in spotting enemy spies. Just in case the invaders manage to breach your defenses, you will want to have a secret hideout to keep your valuable treasures safe. Back up your important data regularly, so even if the bad guys steal or damage something, you can still retrieve it from your hidden stash.

Install security cameras and alarms around your castle to alert you if there is any sign of trouble. Similarly, use security software to monitor your digital spaces for any suspicious activity that could indicate a cyber-attack. Have a plan in place for what to do if your castle comes under attack. Just like knights would call for reinforcements if they were outnumbered, you should have a team ready to respond quickly and effectively to any cyber threats. Just as knights trained regularly to stay sharp, you need to keep up with the latest tactics used by cyber-criminals. Stay informed about new threats and defenses so you are always one step ahead of the invaders.

Stay Updated with Tech Trends:

Make it a habit to regularly check reputable tech news websites such as TechCrunch, Wired, The Verge, and Ars Technica. These sites often cover a wide range of topics, from emerging technologies to industry trends and product launches. Subscribe to tech-focused newsletters or RSS feeds to receive curated updates directly in your inbox or feed reader. This way, you will stay informed without having to actively seek out news. Consider setting up Google Alerts for specific keywords related to your interests or industry. This way, you will receive notifications whenever there is news or articles related to those keywords.

Keep an eye out for tech events and conferences happening locally or globally. Major events like CES (Consumer Electronics Show),

Mobile World Congress, and Google I/O often showcase the latest innovations and trends. Many conferences offer virtual attendance options, making it easier to participate from anywhere in the world. Take advantage of these opportunities to access valuable insights and network with industry professionals. Do not overlook smaller, niche events focused on specific technologies or industries. These events can provide deeper dives into topics of interest and opportunities for more meaningful interactions.

Participate in online communities and forums relevant to your interests or industry. Platforms like Reddit, Stack Overflow, and GitHub host vibrant communities where you can ask questions, share knowledge, and stay updated on the latest developments. Engage in discussions, contribute your own insights, and learn from the experiences of others. Building connections within these communities can provide valuable opportunities for collaboration and knowledge-sharing. Consider joining professional organizations or industry associations related to your field. These organizations often host events, webinars, and networking opportunities that can help you stay informed and connected.

Identify key figures in your industry or areas of interest and follow them on social media platforms like LinkedIn, Twitter, and Medium. Industry leaders, influencers, and experts often share valuable insights, opinions, and predictions about tech trends. Engage with their content by liking, commenting, and sharing posts that resonate with you. This can help you build relationships with thought leaders and stay connected with the broader tech community. Consider subscribing to podcasts or

YouTube channels hosted by industry experts. These platforms often feature in-depth discussions and interviews with leaders in the tech space, providing additional perspectives and insights.

Take a hands-on approach to learning by experimenting with new technologies and tools. Set aside time to explore different software applications, programming languages, or hardware devices that pique your interest. Consider participating in hackathons, coding challenges, or open-source projects to gain practical experience and collaborate with others in the tech community. Do not be afraid to step out of your comfort zone and try new things.

Take advantage of online learning platforms like Coursera, Udemy, and edX to access courses and training programs on a wide range of tech-related topics. Identify areas where you'd like to deepen your knowledge or acquire new skills and search for courses that align with your learning objectives. Look for courses taught by reputable instructors with real-world experience in their respective fields. Read reviews and course descriptions carefully to ensure they meet your needs and expectations. Set aside dedicated time for learning and commit to completing courses or certifications. Stay organized and track your progress as you work through the material.

Chapter 15

Customer Relationship Management

Your business is like a ship sailing through stormy seas, and your customers are the guiding stars that light your way. Customer Relationship Management (CRM) is not just about managing contacts or tracking sales – it is about building meaningful connections with the people who fuel your business's success. It is about understanding their needs, anticipating their desires, and delivering experiences that leave them coming back for more. Mastering the art of CRM is essential for exploring the ever-changing tides of customer preferences and expectations. So, let's set sail on this journey together and discover how the power of CRM can transform your business into a beacon of customer satisfaction and loyalty.

Building Customer Trust

The cornerstone of any successful business is customer trust. Imagine it as the sturdy foundation upon which your entrepreneurial dreams are built. Without it, your business is like a ship without a rudder, adrift in a sea of uncertainty. Establishing and maintaining trust with your customers is not just important – it is absolutely vital. It is the bedrock of long-lasting relationships, repeat business, and positive word-of-mouth referrals. So, how can you earn the trust of your customers and keep it strong? Here are some tried-and-true strategies to help you build and maintain customer trust:

Deliver on Your Promises: Nothing builds trust faster than delivering on your promises – every single time. From meeting deadlines to honoring warranties or providing exceptional customer service, consistency is key. Be honest and transparent in your communications, and always follow through on your commitments.

Prioritize Customer Satisfaction: Make it your mission to delight your customers at every touchpoint. Listen to their feedback, address their concerns promptly, and go above and beyond to exceed their expectations. Show them that their satisfaction is your top priority, and they will reward you with their trust and loyalty.

Be Authentic and Genuine: Authenticity breeds trust, so be genuine in your interactions with customers. Do not try to be something you are not or make promises you can't keep. Instead, be real, honest, and sincere in your communications, and let your genuine passion for your business shine through.

Provide Social Proof: Showcasing positive reviews, testimonials, and case studies can help instill confidence in your brand and build trust with prospective customers. Encourage satisfied customers to share their experiences publicly on social media, review sites, or your website. Authentic, user-generated content is incredibly powerful in building trust and credibility.

Protect Customer Privacy and Data: In today's digital age, protecting customer privacy and data is paramount. Be transparent about how you collect, use, and protect customer information and adhere to strict data privacy regulations. Invest in robust cybersecurity measures to safeguard sensitive data and reassure customers that their information is safe in your hands.

Build Long-Term Relationships: Trust is built over time through consistent, positive interactions. Focus on building long-term relationships with your customers rather than pursuing short-term gains. Invest in personalized communication, loyalty programs, and ongoing support to nurture customer relationships and foster trust and loyalty.

Admit Mistakes and Take Responsibility: Nobody's perfect, and mistakes happen. When they do, own up to them, apologize sincerely, and take swift action to make things right. Customers appreciate honesty and accountability, and admitting mistakes can actually strengthen trust by demonstrating your commitment to integrity and transparency.

Strategies for clear and persuasive communication.

Communication is the bridge that connects you to your customers, allowing you to understand their needs, address their concerns, and forge meaningful connections. As an entrepreneur, mastering the art of clear and persuasive communication is essential for earning the trust and loyalty of your customers. It is not just about what you say but how you say it – the tone, the timing, and the authenticity of your message all play a crucial role in building rapport and fostering positive relationships. So, let's dive into some strategies to help you communicate with your customers in a way that resonates and inspires action:

Listen First, Speak Second: Effective communication begins with listening. Take the time to truly understand your customers' needs, preferences, and pain points before jumping in with your own message.

Ask open-ended questions, actively listen to their responses, and show genuine empathy and interest in what they have to say.

Speak Their Language: Tailor your communication style and messaging to resonate with your target audience. Use language that is clear, concise, and relatable, avoiding jargon or technical terms that may confuse or alienate your customers. Speak in terms of benefits and solutions rather than features, focusing on how your product or service can address their specific needs and pain points.

Provide Value in Every Interaction: Make every communication with your customers count by providing value at every touchpoint. Provide helpful tips and advice, personalized recommendations or exclusive offers and promotions, aim to enrich your customers' lives and experiences through your communication efforts.

Be Responsive and Accessible: Timeliness is key when it comes to communication. Be responsive to customer inquiries, feedback, and concerns and strive to provide prompt and helpful responses. Make it easy for customers to reach you through multiple channels – phone, email, social media, or live chat – and be proactive in addressing their needs and resolving issues.

Use Visuals and Storytelling: Visuals can be incredibly powerful in conveying your message and capturing your customers' attention. Use compelling imagery, videos, and graphics to complement your written communication and bring your brand story to life. Incorporate storytelling techniques to engage and inspire your audience, weaving narratives that resonate emotionally and leave a lasting impression.

Communication is a two-way street, so do not forget to seek feedback from your customers and use it to continuously improve your communication efforts. Encourage customers to share their thoughts, opinions, and suggestions and use their feedback to refine your messaging, products, and services over time.

Handling Customer Complaints

Handling customer complaints is like turning a challenging puzzle into a masterpiece – it requires patience, creativity, and a knack for problem-solving. Rather than seeing complaints as roadblocks, savvy entrepreneurs view them as opportunities to showcase their commitment to customer satisfaction and turn negative feedback into positive outcomes. Here is how you can transform customer complaints into valuable learning experiences and opportunities for growth:

Listen with Empathy: When a customer reaches out with a complaint, it is essential to listen attentively and empathetically. Let them express their concerns without interruption and validate their feelings by acknowledging their frustrations. Show genuine empathy and understanding and reassure them that their feedback is valued and taken seriously.

Apologize and Take Responsibility: A sincere apology can go a long way in diffusing tension and rebuilding trust. Take ownership of the issue, even if it was not directly your fault, and apologize for any inconvenience or dissatisfaction experienced by the customer. Avoid making excuses or shifting blame – instead, focus on finding a resolution and making things right.

Investigate and Understand the Root Cause: Dig deeper to understand the root cause of the complaint and identify any underlying issues or patterns that may need addressing. Gather relevant information from the customer, your team, and your processes to gain a comprehensive understanding of the situation. Analyze the feedback objectively and use it as an opportunity to uncover areas for improvement.

Communicate Transparently: Keep the lines of communication open with the customer throughout the resolution process. Provide regular updates on the status of their complaint and be transparent about the steps you are taking to address their concerns. Be honest about any limitations or challenges you may encounter along the way and set realistic expectations for resolution.

Offer a Solution or Compensation: Once you have identified the root cause of the complaint, work proactively to find a solution that meets the customer's needs and expectations. Offer compensation or restitution where appropriate through a refund, a discount on future purchases, or a complimentary upgrade or service. Demonstrate your commitment to customer satisfaction by going above and beyond to make things right.

Learn and Improve: Every customer complaint is an opportunity to learn and improve your business processes. Take the feedback to heart and use it to drive positive change within your organization. Implement corrective actions to address systemic issues, train your team on best practices for handling complaints, and continuously monitor and evaluate customer feedback to ensure ongoing improvement.

Follow-Up and Express Gratitude: After the complaint has been resolved, follow up with the customer to ensure their satisfaction and express gratitude for their patience and understanding. Thank them for bringing the issue to your attention and reassure them that their feedback has been invaluable in helping you improve your products or services. Leave a positive, lasting impression by showing genuine appreciation for their business.

Personalizing Customer Experience

In today's competitive business landscape, offering a one-size-fits-all approach simply won't cut it. Customers crave individualized attention and solutions that cater to their unique needs and preferences. As an entrepreneur, personalizing the customer experience is not just a nice-to-have – it is a must-have for building strong, lasting relationships and driving customer loyalty. Here is how you can tailor your services to meet the needs of each customer:

Get to Know Your Customers: Take the time to truly understand your customers – their demographics, preferences, purchase history, and pain points. Use customer relationship management (CRM) tools and analytics to gather data and insights that enable you to create detailed customer profiles. The more you know about your customers, the better equipped you will be to personalize their experience.

Segment Your Audience: Not all customers are the same, so it is essential to segment your audience based on common characteristics or behaviors. Divide your customer base into distinct segments: by demographics, buying habits, or interests to tailor your marketing messages, offers, and experiences to each group's specific needs and preferences.

Offer Personalized Recommendations: Use the data you have collected to provide personalized product recommendations and suggestions to each customer. Through targeted email campaigns, personalized website content, or in-store recommendations, offer suggestions based on past purchases, browsing history, or similar customers' preferences. By anticipating their needs and interests, you can enhance the shopping experience and drive additional sales.

Provide Customized Communication: Tailor your communication to each customer's preferred channels, frequency, and messaging style. Some customers may prefer email updates, while others may prefer SMS or social media messages. Pay attention to their communication preferences and respect their boundaries to ensure a positive experience. Personalize your messaging to address them by name and speak directly to their needs and interests.

Deliver Exceptional Customer Service: Personalization extends beyond marketing and sales — it is also about delivering exceptional customer service that exceeds expectations. Train your team to provide personalized assistance and support through proactive outreach, tailored recommendations, or personalized solutions to customer inquiries or issues. Show customers that you value their business and are committed to meeting their needs.

Collect and Act on Feedback: Solicit feedback from your customers regularly and use it to continually refine and improve your personalized offerings. Pay attention to customer comments, reviews, and suggestions and use them to identify areas for enhancement or new opportunities for personalization. Demonstrate that you are listening and responsive to customer feedback by implementing changes based on their input.

Chapter 16
Scaling Your Business

As Andrew Grove, the co-founder of Intel, famously said, "***Only the paranoid survives.***" Knowing when to scale your business is like navigating a ship through uncharted waters – it requires foresight, strategy, and a keen sense of timing. As an entrepreneur, recognizing the right moment to scale can mean the difference between stagnation and exponential growth. It's about striking the delicate balance between ambition and pragmatism, seizing opportunities while mitigating risks. Scaling at the right time allows you to capitalize on market demand, expand your reach, and unlock new revenue streams. However, scaling prematurely can lead to overextension, resource depletion, and, ultimately, failure. So, how do you know when it's time to scale? It's about closely monitoring key indicators such as customer demand, revenue growth, and operational capacity. When you have validated your business model, established product-market fit, and have the resources and infrastructure in place to support growth, it may be time to take the leap. But remember, scaling is not a one-size-fits-all solution – it requires careful planning, strategic investment, and a willingness to adapt to changing market dynamics.

When and How to Scale?

Scaling a business demands meticulous planning, strategic insight, and a profound grasp of your market dynamics and available resources. Scaling prematurely risks dissipating resources and diluting efficacy, while scaling too conservatively may result in missed opportunities and stunted growth. So, how does one ascertain the opportune moment and method for expansion?

Survey Market Dynamics: Begin by scrutinizing market demand for your offerings. Keep a keen eye on pivotal metrics such as customer inquiries, sales trajectory, and market trends to gauge whether the climate is ripe for expansion. Delve into comprehensive market analysis and competitor scrutiny to discern potential growth avenues and avenues for differentiation.

Assess Financial Viability: Next, conduct a thorough assessment of your financial standing to ascertain if you possess the necessary resources and fiscal stability to sustain growth. Evaluate elements such as revenue momentum, profit margins, cash inflows, and avenues for financing. Scrutinize whether scaling necessitates additional investment and assess the potential returns on such endeavors.

Validate Your Business Model: Prior to scaling, ensure your business model is unequivocally validated and resonates with the market. Subject your product or service to rigorous market testing, solicit feedback from clientele, and refine your offering based on their inputs. Validate your pricing schema, distribution channels, and marketing strategies to ensure their efficacy and scalability.

Cultivate Scalable Infrastructure: Invest in cultivating infrastructure and systems capable of accommodating growth without compromising efficiency or quality. Integrate automation into repetitive tasks, optimize operational workflows and deploy technology solutions amenable to scalability. Lay emphasis on scalability during the nascent stages, structuring your operations with future expansion in mind.

Define Clear Objectives: Articulate clear objectives and milestones for your scaling endeavors and devise a strategic blueprint to attain them. Establish measurable targets such as revenue benchmarks, market penetration objectives, or forays into untapped markets. Fragment your goals into actionable steps and temporal milestones, periodically assessing progress to stay on track.

Track Key Performance Indicators: Monitor pertinent key performance indicators (KPIs) to evaluate the health and efficacy of your business and pinpoint avenues for enhancement. Gauge metrics like customer acquisition costs, lifetime value of clientele, churn rates, and profitability to gauge the effectiveness of your growth initiatives. Harness data-driven insights to drive judicious decision-making and recalibration as necessary.

The Global Perspective of Entrepreneurship

Scaling your business to a global level is not just about expanding your reach; it's about unlocking a world of opportunities and maximizing your impact. By going global, you gain access to new markets, customers, and talent pools, allowing you to diversify and future-proof your business against regional economic fluctuations. Moreover, expanding internationally can significantly increase revenue streams and profitability, as you tap into larger consumer bases and capitalize on economies of scale. Beyond financial gains, scaling globally enables you to establish your brand on a global stage, enhancing credibility and recognition. Additionally, it fosters innovation and cross-cultural collaboration as you engage with diverse perspectives and approaches. Ultimately, scaling your business to a global scale has the potential to create profound and far-reaching impacts, not only on your company's growth trajectory but also on the broader economy and society as a whole.

Understanding Global Markets

When you are considering expanding your business globally, it's crucial to do your homework. This means conducting thorough market research to understand the unique dynamics of each market you are eyeing. Look into trends, consumer preferences, regulatory environments, and even cultural nuances. By understanding these factors, you will be better equipped to tailor your products or services to meet the specific needs of each market, increasing your chances of success.

Adaptability is another key trait to cultivate when exploring international waters. What works in one country may not necessarily work in another. That's why it's important to be flexible and open to adjusting your strategies based on local conditions. This could involve anything from tweaking your pricing strategy to accommodate different economic realities to customizing your marketing campaigns to resonate with local cultural values. The ability to adapt to diverse market environments is essential for thriving in the global marketplace.

Cultural awareness is perhaps one of the most underrated yet crucial aspects of international business. Every culture has its own unique customs, communication styles and business practices. By taking the time to learn about and respect these cultural differences, you can build stronger relationships with international partners and customers. This could be as simple as learning a few key phrases in the local language or understanding the proper etiquette for business meetings. Cultivating cultural sensitivity demonstrates respect for your counterparts and can set you apart from competitors who overlook this important aspect of global business.

Building strategic partnerships with local players is another smart move when expanding internationally. Local partners can provide invaluable insights into the market landscape, help navigate regulatory hurdles, and provide access to key networks and resources. Whether it's finding a reliable distributor, forming a joint venture with a local company, or establishing relationships with government officials, building strong partnerships can significantly accelerate your entry and growth in international markets.

Cultural Sensitivity and Diversity

Embracing cultural sensitivity and diversity within your business is not merely a task to check off a list; it's about cultivating an environment where every individual feels genuinely valued and respected. Here are several strategies to authentically appreciate and integrate diversity:

Cultivate Awareness: Begin by fostering cultural awareness among your team members. Host workshops or training sessions aimed at educating employees on various cultures, customs, and communication nuances. Encourage open dialogue and discussions around diversity and inclusivity in the workplace.

Lead with Integrity: As a leader, it's paramount to lead by example and demonstrate unwavering commitment to diversity and inclusion across all facets of your business. Promote diversity in recruitment practices, advancement opportunities, and decision-making processes. Showcase that you genuinely appreciate diverse viewpoints and contributions.

Establish Inclusive Policies: Scrutinize your company policies and procedures to ensure they are inclusive and accommodating to the needs of every employee, regardless of cultural background. This might entail offering flexible work arrangements, extending language support, or commemorating diverse holidays and cultural observances.

Nurture an Inclusive Environment: Foster an inclusive culture where everyone feels a sense of belonging and respect. Encourage collaborative efforts and teamwork among colleagues from diverse backgrounds. Recognize and celebrate diversity by highlighting each team member's unique talents and contributions.

Provide Cultural Sensitivity Training: Implement cultural sensitivity training programs to equip employees with a deeper understanding and appreciation of cultural differences. Such training can aid in developing empathy, effective communication skills, and conflict-resolution abilities when collaborating with peers from diverse cultural backgrounds.

Seek Varied Perspectives: Actively solicit diverse perspectives and insights in decision-making processes. Encourage team members from diverse cultural backgrounds to share their thoughts and ideas freely. This approach fosters innovation and enhances decision-making outcomes for your business.

Support Employee Resource Groups: Establish platforms like employee resource groups or affinity groups to facilitate connections among employees who share common cultural identities or interests. These groups offer invaluable opportunities for mutual support, camaraderie, and personal growth.

Celebrate Diversity: Lastly, commemorate diversity within your workplace by organizing cultural events, diversity appreciation days, or multicultural gatherings where employees can showcase their cultural heritage through food, music, and traditions. These initiatives not only foster a sense of inclusivity but also foster cross-cultural understanding and appreciation.

Connect with entrepreneurs worldwide

Global networking is essential for entrepreneurs as it opens up a myriad of opportunities for collaboration, learning, and growth on a global scale. Connecting with entrepreneurs worldwide allows you to tap into diverse perspectives, access new markets, and forge valuable partnerships that can propel your business forward. To effectively connect with entrepreneurs worldwide, consider the following strategies:

Attend Global Networking Events: Attend international conferences, trade shows, and networking events that attract entrepreneurs from around the world. These events provide opportunities to meet and connect with like-minded individuals, exchange ideas, and explore potential collaboration opportunities.

Utilize Online Platforms: Join online networking platforms and communities tailored to entrepreneurs, such as LinkedIn groups, industry forums, or virtual networking events. These platforms offer a convenient way to connect with entrepreneurs worldwide, regardless of geographical location.

Join International Associations and Chambers of Commerce: Become a member of international business associations, chambers of commerce, or industry-specific organizations with a global presence. These networks facilitate connections with entrepreneurs and business leaders across different countries and industries.

Utilize Social Media: Leverage social media platforms like Twitter, Facebook, and Instagram to connect with entrepreneurs and thought leaders from around the world. Engage in conversations, share insights, and build relationships with individuals who share common interests or goals.

Seek Referrals and Introductions: Leverage your existing network to seek referrals and introductions to entrepreneurs in other countries. Reach out to colleagues, mentors, or business contacts who may have connections or insights into specific markets or industries of interest.

International Regulations and Compliance

When it comes to running a business on a global scale, exploring international regulations and compliance is absolutely vital. These rules cover everything from trade laws to environmental standards, and not following them can lead to serious consequences like fines or even getting shut down. By staying on top of these regulations, you not only avoid risks but also open up opportunities for growth in new markets. Plus, protecting your intellectual property is key to maintaining your competitive edge. Ultimately, sticking to the rules enhances your reputation and credibility, showing everyone that you are committed to doing business the right way, no matter where you are in the world.

Let's break down the international laws that businesses need to know about. First up, we have got trade laws. These govern how goods and services move between countries. Think tariffs, import/export rules, and trade disputes – all covered by agreements like the World Trade Organization (WTO) and regional trade deals. Next, we have intellectual property laws. This is all about protecting your ideas, trademarks, and creative works. International agreements like TRIPS set the standards here to make sure your innovations and brands are safe from unauthorized use.

Moving on to labor laws. These regulations set the standards for things like wages, working conditions, and non-discrimination. Bodies like the International Labour Organization lay down the rules to ensure fair treatment for workers worldwide. Environmental laws are up next. These govern how businesses impact the planet – covering pollution, conservation, and sustainable development. Treaties like the Kyoto Protocol and the Paris Agreement set targets to protect the environment and promote sustainability.

Antitrust laws are another key area. These laws aim to keep markets fair and competitive by preventing anti-competitive practices. Organizations like UNCTAD and OECD work to promote fair competition globally. Last but not least, we have got data protection and privacy laws. These regulations govern how businesses handle personal data. The GDPR is a big one here, setting the standard for data protection and privacy rights across the EU. To navigate international regulations and compliance effectively, businesses should:

Conduct Comprehensive Due Diligence: Conduct thorough due diligence to understand the regulatory requirements and legal obligations applicable to their business operations in different countries. This may involve consulting legal experts, regulatory authorities, or industry associations to ensure compliance with relevant laws and regulations.

Implement Robust Compliance Programs: Develop and implement robust compliance programs to ensure ongoing adherence to international regulations. These programs should include policies, procedures, and controls designed to identify, prevent, and mitigate compliance risks effectively. Training and awareness programs should also be provided to employees to promote a culture of compliance within the organization.

Stay Informed and Updated: Stay informed about changes to international regulations and compliance requirements that may impact business operations. Monitor regulatory developments, legislative changes, and industry standards to ensure timely compliance with evolving regulatory landscapes.

Maintain Accurate Records: Maintain accurate records and documentation to demonstrate compliance with international regulations. This includes keeping detailed records of transactions, contracts, permits, licenses, certifications, and other relevant documentation that may be required to demonstrate compliance with regulatory requirements.

Chapter 17
Adapting to Changing Economic Climates

Think of your business as a ship going through different seas—sometimes you will encounter smooth sailing, while other times you will face stormy waters. Now, imagine you have the flexibility and agility to adjust your course as needed, steering clear of obstacles and capitalizing on new opportunities. That's the power of adapting to changing economic climates. Whether it's a sudden downturn in the economy or a shift in consumer behavior, being able to adapt quickly and effectively can mean the difference between sinking or sailing ahead. By staying attuned to market trends, diversifying your revenue streams, and remaining agile in your decision-making, you can navigate through economic ups and downs with confidence, ensuring the long-term success and sustainability of your business.

Economic Awareness

Consider the impact of economic fluctuations on a business using the example of a local eatery named "Flavorful Bites." During periods of economic upturns, "Flavorful Bites" thrives with a bustling crowd of dinner, enjoying its delectable dishes and welcoming atmosphere. However, when economic conditions take a downturn, patrons may tighten their spending habits, opting for more economical dining options or preparing meals at home. Consequently, "Flavorful Bites" experiences a decline in customer traffic and revenue. To navigate these economic changes, the restaurant proprietor might implement strategies such as offering enticing deals or adjusting the menu to feature more budget-friendly selections. Additionally, exploring delivery or takeout services could help reach customers who prefer dining at home during uncertain economic times. By remaining adaptable and attuned to economic shifts, "Flavorful Bites" can endure fluctuations and maintain its status as a beloved culinary destination within the community.

Whether it's shifts in consumer behavior, fluctuations in market demand, or alterations in government policies, economic changes can deeply influence your operations and bottom line. By staying attuned to economic trends within your industry and beyond, you can anticipate challenges and opportunities, enabling you to take timely actions to adapt and thrive. Whether it's adjusting your pricing strategies, diversifying your revenue streams, or investing in innovation, proactive responses to economic shifts can bolster your resilience and competitiveness in the market. Therefore, as entrepreneurs, it's crucial to remain vigilant, continuously monitor economic indicators, and leverage this knowledge to make informed decisions that propel your business forward, even amidst uncertainty.

Crisis Management

These challenging times call for proactive strategies to navigate through the storm and come out stronger on the other side. Here is how we can tackle this together:

- **Assess the Situation**: It's crucial to understand how the economic downturn may affect our business. Let's analyze the current situation and assess potential risks and opportunities.

- **Preserve Cash Flow:** Cash is king during tough times. We will need to tighten our belts and find ways to conserve cash while ensuring we have enough liquidity to keep the business running smoothly.

- **Diversify Revenue Streams**: Let's explore new avenues to generate revenue and reduce our reliance on any single source. This could involve offering new products or services, targeting different market segments, or exploring new distribution channels.

- **Focus on Core Competencies**: We should double down on what we do best and focus our resources on our core competencies. By concentrating on our strengths, we can maintain our competitive edge and weather the downturn more effectively.

- **Maintain Customer Relationships**: Our customers are our lifeline, so let's prioritize nurturing those relationships. We will need to provide exceptional value, personalized service, and flexible solutions to meet their evolving needs.

- **Adapt and Innovate:** Flexibility and innovation are key to surviving and thriving in challenging times. Let's stay agile and open-minded, embracing change and exploring new ways to serve our customers better.

- Invest in Talent and Technology: Our team is our greatest asset, so let's invest in their development and leverage technology to enhance productivity and efficiency.

- Seeking Financial Support: We should not hesitate to seek financial assistance if needed. Whether it's through government programs, loans, or other forms of funding, let's explore all available options to support our business.

- Communicating Transparently: Transparency is essential during times of uncertainty. Let's keep our stakeholders informed about our challenges, strategies and progress, building trust and confidence along the way.

- Staying Resilient and Optimistic: Finally, let's stay positive and resilient in the face of adversity. By maintaining a can-do attitude and focusing on solutions rather than problems, we can overcome any obstacle that comes our way. Together, we will navigate through this economic downturn and emerge stronger than ever before.

Adapting business models to changing economic scenarios.

Dealing with changing economic scenarios is a critical aspect of entrepreneurship, requiring adaptability and strategic foresight. As entrepreneurs, we must remain vigilant in assessing market dynamics and proactively adjust our business models to align with prevailing economic conditions. This process begins with a thorough evaluation of the economic landscape, encompassing factors such as consumer behavior, market trends, and macroeconomic indicators. By understanding the broader economic context, we can anticipate potential challenges and opportunities, empowering us to make informed decisions about our business strategies.

Once we have a clear understanding of the economic climate, it's essential to identify areas within our business model that may require adjustment. This could involve reassessing our pricing strategies to remain competitive in a downturn, diversifying our product or service offerings to meet changing consumer needs, or exploring new revenue streams to offset declines in traditional sources of income. Embracing flexibility and innovation is key during this process, as it allows us to explore new approaches and experiment with different strategies to adapt to evolving market conditions.

Technology plays a pivotal role in enabling business model adaptation, offering tools and solutions to streamline operations, enhance customer experiences, and drive growth. Whether it's implementing e-commerce platforms to reach a broader audience, leveraging data analytics to gain insights into consumer preferences, or embracing automation to improve efficiency, technology can empower us to navigate changing economic landscapes with agility and resilience. By harnessing the power of technology, we can stay ahead of the curve and position our businesses for success in an ever-evolving marketplace.

Building strong relationships within our network is also essential for adapting our business models to changing economic scenarios. Collaborating with customers, suppliers, and industry peers allows us to gain valuable insights, share best practices, and identify emerging trends that may impact our businesses. By fostering a spirit of collaboration and communication, we can leverage the collective knowledge and experience of our network to navigate through economic challenges and capitalize on new opportunities.

Financial Planning for Uncertainty

To navigate unpredictable economic conditions, you need to adopt a comprehensive approach to financial preparedness. This approach includes the following steps:

Emergency Fund Essentials: Establishing an emergency fund is akin to creating a safety net for your business. This fund should ideally cover at least three to six months' worth of essential business expenses, including rent, utilities, payroll, and other operational costs. By setting aside these funds, you create a buffer that can help tide your business over during lean periods or unforeseen emergencies.

Cash Flow Vigilance: Cash flow management is paramount for businesses of all sizes, but it becomes especially crucial during uncertain economic times. Monitoring cash flow close involves tracking incoming and outgoing funds to ensure that your business maintains sufficient liquidity to cover its obligations. Strategies for optimizing cash flow include incentivizing early payments from customers, negotiating favorable payment terms with suppliers, and implementing stringent credit control measures.

Revenue Diversity: Relying too heavily on a single source of revenue can leave your business vulnerable to economic fluctuations or disruptions in the market. Diversifying your revenue streams involves exploring alternative markets, expanding your product or service offerings, or targeting new customer segments. By diversifying your revenue sources, you can spread risk and minimize the impact of downturns in any particular market or industry sector.

Cost-Cutting Measures: Controlling costs is essential for maintaining financial stability, especially during challenging economic conditions. Conduct a thorough review of your business expenses and identify areas where costs can be reduced or eliminated without compromising quality or efficiency. This may involve renegotiating contracts with suppliers, streamlining operations, or exploring opportunities for outsourcing non-core functions.

Financing Safeguards: Access to additional capital can provide a lifeline for businesses facing financial challenges. Explore various financing options, such as business loans, lines of credit, or equity investment, to bolster your financial resources when needed. Having a financial safety net in place can provide peace of mind and ensure that your business has the resources it needs to weather unexpected downturns or seize growth opportunities.

Scenario Planning: Anticipating potential economic scenarios and developing contingency plans is essential for business resilience. Conduct scenario planning exercises to assess the potential impact of various economic scenarios on your business and identify strategies to mitigate risks and capitalize on opportunities. This proactive approach allows you to be prepared for whatever challenges may arise and enables you to respond effectively to changing market conditions.

Credit Health Maintenance: Maintaining a strong credit profile is essential for ensuring access to financing and other financial resources when needed. Stay on top of your financial obligations, pay bills on time, and manage debt responsibly to preserve your creditworthiness.

Regularly review your credit report to identify any inaccuracies or issues that need to be addressed and take steps to rectify them promptly.

Professional Guidance: Seeking advice from financial experts, accountants, or business mentors can provide valuable insights and guidance on managing your finances effectively during uncertain economic times. These professionals can offer strategic advice, help you identify opportunities for improvement, and provide support and guidance as you navigate through challenging economic conditions.

Handling Competition in Business

In today's fiercely competitive world, entrepreneurship demands more than just a good idea—it requires resilience, adaptability, and a strategic mindset to thrive amidst rivals. The business landscape is constantly evolving, with new players entering the market and existing ones vying for dominance. As entrepreneurs, we must equip ourselves with the tools and skills needed to navigate this competitive environment effectively. This means staying abreast of industry trends, understanding our competitors' strengths and weaknesses, and continuously innovating to stay ahead of the curve. By embracing competition as a driving force for growth and improvement, entrepreneurs can turn challenges into opportunities and carve out their own path to success in the dynamic world of business.

Understanding what competitors are doing right and wrong

Analyzing competitors is a multifaceted process that requires a thorough understanding of the competitive landscape and a keen eye for detail. To begin, entrepreneurs must identify their direct and indirect competitors—the businesses that offer similar products or services to the same target market. This involves conducting market research, using tools like industry reports, online databases, and social media platforms to gather information about competitors' offerings, market positioning, and customer demographics.

Once competitors have been identified, entrepreneurs can delve deeper into analyzing their strategies, strengths, and weaknesses. This involves examining various aspects of competitors' businesses, including their product or service features, pricing strategies, distribution channels, marketing tactics, and customer reviews. By comparing these factors to their own business, entrepreneurs can gain valuable insights into what competitors are doing right and where they may be falling short.

Understanding competitors' strengths allows entrepreneurs to identify areas where they can improve or differentiate their own offerings. For example, if a competitor is known for their excellent customer service, entrepreneurs can prioritize enhancing their own customer support to remain competitive. Similarly, analyzing competitors' weaknesses can highlight potential opportunities for entrepreneurs to capitalize on gaps in the market or address unmet customer needs. For instance, if a competitor has limited product availability or a poor online presence, entrepreneurs can focus on expanding their product range or improving their digital marketing efforts to gain a competitive advantage.

Moreover, ongoing monitoring of competitors is essential to stay abreast of changes in the market and adapt strategies accordingly. This involves regularly tracking competitors' activities, such as new product launches, pricing adjustments, marketing campaigns, and customer feedback. By staying vigilant and responsive to changes in the competitive landscape, entrepreneurs can position themselves more effectively and make informed decisions to drive business growth.

Standing out in a crowded market

Making your business stand out among competitors requires a combination of differentiation, innovation, and effective marketing strategies. Here is how you can achieve this:

- **Unique Value Proposition (UVP):** Define what sets your business apart from competitors by identifying your unique value proposition. This could be based on factors such as product quality, exceptional customer service, competitive pricing, or innovative features. Highlighting your UVP in your marketing materials and communications helps differentiate your brand and attract customers.

- **Innovation**: Continuously innovate and adapt to meet changing customer needs and market trends. This could involve introducing new products or services, improving existing offerings, or leveraging technology to enhance customer experiences. Innovation demonstrates your commitment to staying ahead of the curve and positions your business as a leader in your industry.

- **Exceptional Customer Service**: Provide exceptional customer service that goes above and beyond expectations. Respond promptly to customer inquiries and concerns, personalize interactions, and strive to exceed customer satisfaction. Positive word-of-mouth referrals and customer reviews can significantly enhance your reputation and set your business apart from competitors.

- **Branding and Storytelling**: Develop a strong brand identity and tell a compelling brand story that resonates with your target audience. Use branding elements such as logos, colors, and messaging consistently across all marketing channels to create brand recognition and loyalty. Authentic storytelling helps humanize your brand and connect with customers on an emotional level.

- **Marketing Differentiation**: Implement creative and targeted marketing strategies to differentiate your business from competitors. This could include niche targeting, influencer partnerships, experiential marketing events, or guerrilla marketing tactics. Find innovative ways to reach and engage your target audience and communicate your unique value proposition effectively.

- **Focus on Quality**: Emphasize quality in all aspects of your business, from product design and manufacturing to customer service and after-sales support. Consistently delivering high-quality products and services builds trust and credibility with customers, setting your business apart as a reliable and reputable choice.

- **Build Relationships**: Foster strong relationships with customers, suppliers, industry influencers, and other stakeholders. Engage with your audience on social media, participate in industry events and networking opportunities, and collaborate with complementary businesses to expand your reach and enhance your brand visibility.

Using competition as a motivator for improvement

The competition serves as a powerful catalyst for improvement, driving businesses to innovate, evolve, and continually raise the bar. When businesses face competition, they are compelled to strive for excellence in their products, services, and customer experiences to stand out in the marketplace. The pressure to differentiate themselves from competitors pushes businesses to identify areas for enhancement, whether it's through product innovation, process optimization, or customer service excellence. Moreover, competition fosters a culture of continuous learning and adaptation, as businesses must stay agile and responsive to changing market dynamics to maintain their competitive edge. Ultimately, competition motivates businesses to push beyond their limits, challenge the status quo, and pursue excellence in all aspects of their operations.

Collaborative Opportunities

Collaborating with competitors—sounds counterintuitive, right? But believe it or not, it can actually be a smart move for your business. Picture this: by teaming up with your rivals, you can achieve common goals more efficiently. How? Well, think of joint ventures or partnerships where both parties bring their strengths to the table to tackle challenges and seize opportunities together.

Now, here is the exciting part: collaborating with competitors can open up new doors to reach more customers. Imagine forming strategic partnerships to tap into each other's customer bases. It's like expanding your reach and attracting new customers without doing all the heavy lifting alone. Cool, right? And you can do this through cross-promotion, joint marketing campaigns or even referral agreements to boost each other's businesses. But wait, there is more! Collaboration also sparks innovation and knowledge sharing. By teaming up on research projects or participating in industry associations, competitors can fuel a culture of innovation that benefits everyone. It's like leveling up the game for the whole industry.

Now, how do you actually collaborate with competitors? Well, it starts with open communication and building relationships. Look for areas where you can both benefit from working together, whether it's sharing resources, co-developing products, or even teaming up on a marketing campaign. Remember, it's all about finding common ground and seizing opportunities to grow together. So, if you are ready to take your business to the next level, consider the potential of collaborating with your competitors. Who knows? It might just be the strategic move that sets you apart and propels you to success in your industry.

The Importance of Consistency

"In essence, if we want to direct our lives, we must take control of our consistent actions. It's not what we do once in a while that shapes our lives, but what we do consistently."

- Tony Robbins

Consistency is the cornerstone of success in entrepreneurship. It's not about making one big splash or hitting a home run once in a while; rather, it's about showing up day in and day out, consistently putting in the effort, and taking action toward your goals. Consistency breeds trust, reliability, and credibility—qualities that are essential for building strong relationships with customers, investors, and stakeholders. Whether it's delivering high-quality products or services, maintaining a strong brand presence, or staying true to your values and mission, consistency is what sets successful entrepreneurs apart. It's the daily habits, routines, and rituals that compound over time to yield significant results. By committing to consistency in your actions, you create a solid foundation for long-term success and sustainability in entrepreneurship.

Routine and Discipline

Routine and discipline are powerful tools that can significantly impact your success in entrepreneurship. Establishing productive routines and discipline is essential for maintaining focus, increasing productivity, and achieving your goals. To harness the power of routine and discipline, start by defining your goals and priorities. Identify the tasks and activities that are most important for moving your business forward. Then, create a daily or weekly schedule that allocates dedicated time for these tasks. Consistency is key here—stick to your schedule and make your routine a non-negotiable part of your day. Next, cultivate discipline by setting clear boundaries and adhering to them. This may involve setting specific work hours, minimizing distractions, and avoiding procrastination. Practice self-control and willpower, especially when faced with temptations or obstacles that threaten to derail your progress.

Incorporate healthy habits into your routine to support your overall well-being and productivity. This includes prioritizing adequate sleep, exercise, and nutrition, as well as incorporating relaxation and downtime to recharge your energy levels. Additionally, leverage tools and technologies to streamline your workflow and maximize efficiency. Use productivity apps, time management techniques, and project management tools to stay organized, track progress, and stay on track with your goals.

Finally, stay adaptable and flexible in your approach. Recognize that routines may need to be adjusted as circumstances change or new priorities emerge. Embrace a growth mindset and view setbacks or challenges as opportunities for learning and improvement.

Maintaining a consistent brand image

Consistent branding and messaging serve as the backbone of your brand's identity and reputation. They create a cohesive and unified image that resonates with your audience across all channels and touchpoints. This consistency reinforces brand recognition and fosters trust and credibility with your audience as they come to associate your brand with a specific set of values, personality traits, and visual elements. To maintain this consistency, it's essential to start by defining your brand identity. This involves clarifying your brand values, determining your brand's personality, and establishing visual elements such as your logo, colors, and fonts. Once you have a clear understanding of your brand identity, ensure that these elements are consistently applied across all marketing materials, from your website and social media profiles to advertising campaigns and product packaging. Additionally, develop clear and concise brand messaging that effectively communicates your unique value proposition and resonates with your target audience. Use consistent language, tone, and voice across all communications to reinforce your brand identity and build brand consistency. Regularly review and audit your branding and messaging to identify any inconsistencies and make necessary adjustments to maintain a cohesive and unified brand image. By prioritizing consistent branding and messaging, you strengthen your brand identity, enhance brand recognition, and cultivate long-lasting relationships with your audience based on trust and credibility. To keep your audience engaged for consistent branding, you can employ several strategies:

- **Create Compelling Content:** Develop content that is relevant, valuable, and engaging for your audience. This can include informative blog posts, entertaining videos, interactive quizzes, or visually appealing graphics. Ensure that your content aligns with your brand identity and messaging to maintain consistency.

- **Utilize Multiple Channels:** Reach your audience across various channels, including social media platforms, email newsletters, your website, and offline channels like events or print materials. Tailor your content and messaging to each channel while maintaining a cohesive brand identity throughout.

- **Foster Two-Way Communication**: Encourage interaction and feedback from your audience by responding to comments, messages, and reviews promptly. This shows that you value their input and strengthens the relationship between your brand and your audience.

- **Offer Value-Added Services**: Provide additional value to your audience beyond your products or services. This could include educational resources, exclusive discounts, or access to special events or webinars. By offering valuable content and experiences, you can keep your audience engaged and invested in your brand.

- **Personalize Your Interactions**: Use data and insights to personalize your communications and tailor them to the specific interests and preferences of your audience segments. Personalization helps create a more meaningful and relevant experience for your audience, increasing engagement and loyalty.

- **Stay Active and Responsive:** Regularly update your content and engage with your audience to stay top-of-mind. Be proactive in addressing any questions, concerns, or feedback from your audience, showing that you are attentive and responsive to their needs.

By implementing these strategies, you can keep your audience engaged and invested in your brand, fostering long-term relationships and promoting consistent branding.

Steady Growth and Development

Imagine you have two businesses—one that's consistently growing at a stable pace and another that's experiencing rapid, unpredictable growth. The first business focuses on gradual and stable growth, making steady progress over time without overextending itself. It's like building a house brick by brick, ensuring each foundation is solid before adding more. On the other hand, the second business is like a rollercoaster ride—it experiences rapid spikes in growth followed by sudden downturns, making it hard to predict or manage. Now, think about the challenges each business might face. The first business, with its steady growth, can better manage its resources, adapt to market changes, and maintain a strong foundation for long-term success. Meanwhile, the second business might struggle with instability, resource shortages, and a lack of sustainability. By focusing on gradual and stable growth, you are laying the groundwork for sustainable profitability and resilience, setting your business up for success in the long run.

Chapter 18
Entrepreneurial Mindset and Attitudes

"Whether you think you can or you think you can't — you are right."

-Henry Ford

This quote encapsulates the essence of the entrepreneurial mindset and attitude. It's about belief, determination, and a relentless drive to turn vision into reality. An entrepreneurial mindset is marked by a willingness to embrace challenges as opportunities, to take calculated risks, and to persist in the face of adversity. It's not just about starting a business; it's a way of approaching life with curiosity, creativity, and a bias towards action. This mindset is crucial for success in any endeavor, as it fosters innovation, resilience, and a proactive approach to problem-solving. In this chapter, we will delve deeper into the strategies and techniques to cultivate and strengthen this invaluable mindset, empowering you to navigate the complexities of entrepreneurship with confidence and clarity.

Cultivate a positive outlook towards challenges.

So, picture this: you are on your entrepreneurial journey, right? Challenges pop up left and right, and how you deal with them can make all the difference. It's like this: having a positive mindset during tough times is not just a bonus — it's essential for success. When you see obstacles as chances to learn and grow rather than roadblocks, you are already halfway there. This shift in perspective helps you tackle challenges with creativity and resilience, which are like your secret weapons for innovation and problem-solving.

How to cultivate that positive mindset? It's all about being aware of your thoughts and feelings. Do not beat yourself up over frustrations or disappointments – instead, accept them as part of the journey. Knowing that you have got what it takes to overcome obstacles is key to moving forward with determination. Here is another trick: see challenges as opportunities in disguise. Instead of getting stuck on what's going wrong, focus on what you can learn or gain from the situation. Think about it: every hurdle you face is a chance to level up your skills or find new ways to succeed.

And do not forget your support squad! Surround yourself with people who have been there, done that, and can offer guidance and encouragement when you need it most. Sharing experiences with like-minded folks can make tough times feel a whole lot easier. And why not celebrate your wins – no matter how small? Recognizing your progress along the way keeps you motivated and reminds you that you are moving in the right direction. Now, let's talk about failure – it's not the end of the world! Embrace it as part of the learning process. See setbacks as opportunities to grow stronger and wiser, armed with new insights for future success.

A few years ago, I met Sarah, an aspiring entrepreneur in the tech industry, who faced a significant setback in her startup journey when a highly anticipated product feature received a tepid response upon launch. Instead of succumbing to disappointment, Sarah embraced a positive mindset, viewing the setback as an opportunity for growth. With determination and resilience, she and her team listened to user feedback, iterated on the feature, and ultimately succeeded in creating a product that exceeded expectations. Sarah's story underscores the importance of maintaining optimism and resilience in entrepreneurship, showing that setbacks can be turned into stepping stones toward success with the right attitude.

The importance of taking calculated risks

Risk-taking and courage are indispensable components of entrepreneurship, often serving as catalysts for innovation and growth. In the entrepreneurial landscape, taking calculated risks is not merely about blind leaps into the unknown but rather a strategic and informed approach to decision-making. It involves carefully assessing potential outcomes, weighing probabilities, and understanding the potential rewards against the potential losses. Courage, on the other hand, is the willingness to step outside of one's comfort zone, confront uncertainty, and persevere in the face of adversity. Without risk-taking, progress and innovation would be stifled, as entrepreneurs would shy away from venturing into uncharted territory. Moreover, taking calculated risks fosters resilience and adaptability, essential qualities for exploring the dynamic and ever-changing business environment. Ultimately, it is the combination of risk-taking and courage that propels entrepreneurs forward, enabling them to seize opportunities, overcome challenges, and ultimately achieve success in their ventures.

Embrace continuous learning and improvement

The business world moves at lightning speed, with trends shifting, technology evolving, and consumer preferences changing constantly. Staying stuck in one place simply is not an option. That's where continuous learning comes in. It's all about keeping your finger on the pulse, staying updated on what's happening in your industry, and being open to new ideas and approaches. When you approach challenges with a mindset of continual improvement, you are not seeing roadblocks – you are seeing opportunities to learn and grow. Every setback becomes a chance to gather insights that can inform your next move and make your business stronger. Plus, embracing this mindset of constant growth not only drives innovation but also builds resilience. It's like giving yourself a toolkit to navigate the ups and downs of entrepreneurship with confidence. And let's not forget about personal and professional development. By committing to continuous learning, you are investing in yourself, expanding your skills, and becoming a better leader along the way. So, whether you are just starting out or you are a seasoned entrepreneur, remember: the heart of entrepreneurship beats with a commitment to learning and improvement. It's what keeps your business thriving and your mindset positive, no matter what challenges come your way.

Handle negative feedback constructively

Handling negative feedback constructively is a key skill for entrepreneurs, and it starts with maintaining an open mind. When faced with criticism, resist the urge to take it personally and instead approach it with curiosity. Take a moment to understand the root of the feedback and whether there is merit to it. Once you have absorbed the feedback, it's time to take action. Use it as an opportunity to reevaluate your strategies and make necessary adjustments. Do not hesitate to seek input from others to gain different perspectives. When responding to negative feedback, do so professionally and graciously. Acknowledge the feedback, express gratitude for it, and outline your plans for improvement. Finally, do not let negative feedback linger in your mind. Use it as a stepping stone for growth and move forward with confidence, knowing that every piece of feedback, whether positive or negative, contributes to your journey towards success.

Personal Development for Entrepreneurs

"Personal development is not a luxury; it's a necessity for entrepreneurial success,"

-Tony Robbins

Consider the journey of an entrepreneur named Alex. Initially fueled by a groundbreaking idea and boundless enthusiasm, Alex soon encountered the complexities of running a business. Realizing the gaps in his leadership, communication, and time management skills, Alex committed himself to personal development. Through voracious reading, attending workshops, and seeking mentorship, Alex underwent a transformative journey. He emerged as a more effective leader, adept at inspiring his team, articulating his vision, and facing challenges with resilience. Alex's dedication to personal growth not only enhanced his own performance but also propelled his business to new heights. Ultimately, personal development is not just about acquiring skills; it's about unlocking one's full potential as an entrepreneur, enabling individuals like Alex to overcome obstacles, seize opportunities, and leave a lasting mark on their industry.

Understand your strengths and weaknesses

Self-reflection is a powerful tool for raising personal awareness and gaining insights into your strengths and weaknesses as an entrepreneur. To begin, set aside dedicated time for introspection, perhaps at the end of each day or week, to reflect on your experiences, decisions, and interactions. Start by asking yourself probing questions, such as: What were my successes and failures today? What challenges did I face, and how did I handle them? What aspects of my performance could be improved?

Consider seeking feedback from trusted colleagues, mentors, or peers. Their perspectives can provide valuable insights into your blind spots and areas for growth. Be open to constructive criticism and use it as an opportunity to identify patterns or recurring themes in your behavior or decision-making. Once you have identified your strengths and weaknesses, focus on leveraging them to your advantage. Capitalize on your strengths by finding opportunities to showcase and refine them further. Whether it's your creativity, resilience, or ability to communicate effectively, use these strengths to propel yourself forward and differentiate yourself in the marketplace.

Simultaneously, work on addressing your weaknesses through targeted self-improvement efforts. Set specific goals for improvement and develop action plans to address them systematically. Whether it's attending training sessions, seeking mentorship, or practicing new skills, take proactive steps to enhance your capabilities and overcome your limitations. Moreover, consider how you can leverage your strengths to mitigate the impact of your weaknesses. For example, if you excel in strategic thinking but struggle with attention to detail, delegate tasks that require meticulousness to someone who possesses that strength, allowing you to focus on higher-level priorities.

Social Entrepreneurship and Responsibility

Social entrepreneurship is all about using business principles to address social or environmental issues. It's about finding innovative solutions to tackle problems like poverty, inequality, or climate change while still making a profit. Essentially, it's about doing good while doing well. Social entrepreneurs are like superheroes – they are driven by a mission to create positive change in the world, and they are not afraid to think outside the box to make it happen. And when it comes to responsibility, social entrepreneurs take it to the next level. They are not just focused on making money; they are also accountable to their communities, their employees, and the planet. They prioritize things like fair wages, ethical sourcing, and environmental sustainability, ensuring that their businesses have a positive impact every step of the way.

Business with a Cause: Aligning business goals with social impact

Imagine starting a company where your mission is not just about making money but also about making a difference in the world. It's about waking up every morning knowing that your work is contributing to something bigger than yourself – whether it's fighting poverty, protecting the environment, or promoting education.

Take, for example, TOMS Shoes. When Blake Mycoskie founded TOMS, he did not just want to create a successful shoe company; he wanted to help children in need. For every pair of shoes sold, TOMS donates a pair to a child in need. This "one for one" model not only aligns the business's goals with social impact but also resonates deeply with consumers who want to make a difference with their purchases.

Another inspiring example is Patagonia, a company known for its commitment to environmental sustainability. From using recycled materials in its products to donating a portion of its profits to environmental causes, Patagonia's business model is built on the belief that businesses have a responsibility to protect the planet. By aligning its business goals with social and environmental impact, Patagonia has built a loyal customer base and become a leader in the sustainable fashion industry.

Establishing a business with a cause is not always easy. It requires careful planning, dedication, and a willingness to prioritize social impact over short-term profits. But the rewards are immeasurable. Not only do these businesses have the potential to create positive change in the world, but they also have a unique ability to inspire others to join the movement and be part of something bigger than themselves. So, if you are thinking about starting a business, why not consider one with a cause? After all, the world could always use more businesses that are in it for more than just the bottom line.

Sustainable Practices: Implement eco-friendly business strategies

How can businesses contribute to environmental preservation and enhance operational efficiency? Sustainable practices entail implementing eco-friendly strategies across all aspects of business operations. This includes initiatives such as reducing energy consumption, minimizing waste production, and utilizing renewable resources. By integrating sustainable practices into their operations, businesses not only reduce their environmental footprint but also demonstrate a commitment to environmental stewardship. For instance, implementing energy-efficient lighting systems or using recyclable packaging materials not only helps reduce carbon emissions but also results in long-term cost savings. Let's dive into some eco-friendly business practices that can make a positive impact:

- Energy Efficiency: Consider switching to LED lights, upgrading heating and cooling systems, and implementing energy-saving measures to lower your carbon footprint and reduce utility bills.

- Renewable Energy: Explore options like solar or wind power to reduce reliance on fossil fuels and contribute to cleaner energy sources.

- Waste Reduction and Recycling: Start recycling programs, promote reusing materials, and minimize waste generation to lessen environmental impact.

- Sustainable Transportation: Encourage carpooling, biking, or using public transport to reduce emissions associated with commuting.

- Green Procurement: Choose suppliers that prioritize sustainability and offer eco-friendly products and materials.

- Water Conservation: Install water-saving fixtures and implement efficient irrigation systems to conserve water resources.

- Eco-Friendly Office Practices: Embrace paperless workflows, use green cleaning products, and promote telecommuting to minimize environmental impact in the workplace.

- Sustainable Building Design: Incorporate energy-efficient design elements and use sustainable materials in construction projects.

- Carbon Offsetting: Consider investing in carbon offset projects to balance out carbon emissions generated by business activities.

- Environmental Education and Awareness: Provide training on eco-friendly practices and raise awareness among employees and stakeholders about the importance of sustainability.

Community Impact: How businesses can positively impact local communities?

Community impact is all about businesses actively engaging with the people in the neighborhoods they serve. It's about more than just turning a profit—it's about being a part of something bigger, something that benefits everyone involved. Businesses that focus on community impact roll up their sleeves and get involved in local initiatives. Whether it's supporting local charities, sponsoring events, or volunteering time and resources, they are committed to making a positive difference. One powerful way is by providing job opportunities. By hiring locally, businesses not only boost the local economy but also provide valuable employment opportunities for community members. And it's not just about jobs—it's also about offering skills training programs to help people develop and grow in their careers.

Another key aspect of community impact is partnering with local organizations to address social issues. This could mean anything from supporting education programs to tackling homelessness or food insecurity. By working together with community organizations, businesses can leverage their resources and expertise to make a real difference where it's needed most. Take, for example, a restaurant that sources its ingredients from local farmers. Not only does this support the local economy, but it also fosters a sense of community pride and connection among residents. People love knowing that their favorite restaurant is invested in the same community they call home.

Ethical Supply Chains

Ethical supply chains are like the backbone of responsible sourcing and production practices. It's all about making sure that every step of the process, from sourcing raw materials to manufacturing products, is done in a way that respects labor rights, human rights, and the environment. Businesses that prioritize ethical supply chains are not just focused on making a profit—they are committed to making a positive impact on the world around them. Achieving ethical supply chains involves several key steps. First off, businesses need to conduct regular audits of their suppliers to ensure they are meeting ethical standards. This means going beyond just looking at the bottom line and digging deep into how suppliers treat their workers and the environment.

Next, it's all about establishing codes of conduct. These are like guiding principles that set out the expectations for suppliers when it comes to things like fair wages, safe working conditions, and environmental sustainability. By setting clear expectations upfront, businesses can hold their suppliers accountable and ensure everyone is on the same page. But it does not stop there. Transparency and accountability are also crucial. Businesses need to be open and honest about where their products come from and how they are made. This means being upfront with customers and stakeholders about their supply chain practices and actively working to address any issues that arise.

Take, for example, a clothing company that chooses to source materials from suppliers who adhere to fair labor practices and environmentally sustainable production methods. By making this choice, they are not only minimizing the risk of exploitation and environmental harm but also sending a powerful message about their commitment to ethical business practices. So, whether it's through conducting audits, establishing codes of conduct, or promoting transparency and accountability, businesses have a real opportunity to create positive change through ethical supply chains. And by doing so, they are not just building a better business—they are building a better world for everyone.

Strategic Planning and Decision Making

Strategic planning and decision-making are essential pillars of entrepreneurship, providing a roadmap for long-term success and guiding entrepreneurs through the complexities of starting and growing a business. Aspiring entrepreneurs should view strategic planning as an opportunity to clarify their vision, identify potential obstacles, and create a roadmap for achieving their goals. Decision-making, meanwhile, requires entrepreneurs to weigh risks and rewards effectively, making informed choices that align with their long-term vision and objectives. By embracing strategic planning and decision-making as integral parts of the entrepreneurial journey, aspiring entrepreneurs can position themselves for success and navigate the challenges of building a business with confidence and purpose.

Long-term Visioning

Having a long-term vision as an entrepreneur can provide a clear direction for your business and guide your actions toward achieving significant milestones. For instance, let's consider a tech startup aiming to revolutionize renewable energy storage solutions. Their long-term vision might be to become a global leader in sustainable energy technology, providing affordable and scalable solutions to address climate change. With this vision in mind, they can set ambitious but achievable long-term goals, such as developing innovative battery technology, expanding into new markets, and forging strategic partnerships with key industry players. To pursue these goals effectively, the startup can break them down into smaller, actionable steps, develop a timeline for implementation, and regularly review and adjust their strategies based on progress and market conditions. By staying focused on their long-term vision and consistently working towards their goals, the startup can chart a path to success and make a meaningful impact in the renewable energy sector.

Effective Decision-Making Processes

Effective decision-making processes are crucial for entrepreneurs to navigate the complexities of running a business and capitalize on opportunities while minimizing risks. Here are some key steps for entrepreneurs to make sound decisions:

- **Define the Problem**: Clearly identify the issue or opportunity at hand. Break it down into specific components and understand the root cause of the problem or the goal to be achieved.

- **Gather Information:** Collect relevant data, facts, and insights to inform your decision-making process. Consider both quantitative data (such as market research and financial projections) and qualitative information (such as customer feedback and expert opinions).

- **Analyze Options:** Generate multiple potential solutions or courses of action. Evaluate the pros and cons of each option, considering factors like feasibility, cost, potential impact, and alignment with your business goals and values.

- **Consider Alternatives**: Explore alternative approaches and consider potential outcomes under different scenarios. Be open to creative solutions and innovative ideas that may not be immediately obvious.

- **Assess Risks**: Identify and assess potential risks and uncertainties associated with each option. Consider the likelihood of success, as well as any potential negative consequences or unintended side effects.

- **Make the Decision:** Based on your analysis and assessment, make a decision that aligns with your long-term vision and objectives. Trust your instincts, but also rely on logic and evidence to guide your choice.

- **Take Action:** Implement the decision effectively and efficiently. Develop a clear action plan with specific steps, timelines, and responsibilities. Communicate the decision to relevant stakeholders and ensure alignment and buy-in.

- **Evaluate and Adapt**: Monitor the outcomes of your decision and evaluate its effectiveness. Be prepared to adjust your approach if necessary based on feedback and new information. Continuously learn from your experiences and refine your decision-making processes over time.

Analyzing Business Performance

Why is it crucial for entrepreneurs to regularly analyze their business performance? Well, think of it like this: Imagine you are driving a car without a dashboard. How would you know if you are running low on fuel or if the engine temperature is getting too high? Analyzing business performance is like having that dashboard for your business—it gives you real-time insights into how well your business is running and where improvements can be made. How often should you do this? Ideally, it should be done regularly, whether it's monthly, quarterly, or annually, depending on your business's needs. By keeping a close eye on key performance indicators (KPIs) such as sales growth, profitability, customer satisfaction, and operational efficiency, entrepreneurs can track progress toward their goals and make informed decisions to drive success. So, if you want to steer your business in the right direction, regularly analyzing its performance and monitoring KPIs is absolutely essential.

Knowing when and how to change business direction

In the fast-paced world of business, knowing when and how to change direction is essential for staying competitive and relevant. Think of it like sailing a ship: as conditions shift, you need to adjust your course to reach your destination. For example, consider the transformation of Netflix. Originally a DVD rental service, they recognized the growing trend towards online streaming and strategically pivoted their business model. This move allowed them to not only survive but thrive in an evolving market. Similarly, businesses must be vigilant in monitoring market trends, customer needs, and competitive landscapes to identify opportunities for strategic pivots. Whether it's refining product offerings, targeting new markets, or adopting new technologies, businesses that are nimble and adaptable are best positioned to succeed in an ever-changing business environment.

Celebrate Your Entrepreneurial Successes

Entrepreneurs, amidst the whirlwind of running our businesses, it's easy to overlook the importance of celebrating our successes, no matter how small they may seem. Yet, it's crucial to take a step back and acknowledge our achievements, whether it's landing a new client, hitting a sales target, or overcoming a daunting challenge. Celebrating these victories, big or small, not only boosts morale but also serves as a powerful motivator to keep forging ahead. By taking the time to recognize and appreciate our accomplishments, we create a positive and uplifting atmosphere within our teams and fuel the drive to pursue even greater goals. So, let's raise a toast to our triumphs, no matter how humble, and revel in the journey of entrepreneurship—it's these moments of celebration that keep us motivated and inspired as we navigate the highs and lows of business ownership.

Recognize Your Achievements

As entrepreneurs, it's vital to recognize and celebrate the achievements and milestones we reach along our journey. Whether it's securing a new client, launching a successful marketing campaign, or hitting a revenue goal, each accomplishment represents progress and deserves acknowledgment. By taking the time to celebrate these milestones, we not only boost morale within our team but also foster a culture of appreciation and recognition. It's these moments of celebration that keep us motivated, energized, and inspired to continue pushing forward despite the challenges we may face. So, let's pause, acknowledge our achievements, and celebrate the milestones that mark our path to success.

Share Your Success Stories

One of the most powerful ways to inspire others is by sharing your journey and success stories. Whether it's through social media, networking events, or public speaking engagements, sharing your experiences, challenges, and triumphs can motivate and uplift others who are on their entrepreneurial journey. By being transparent about your path to success, you not only inspire others to pursue their dreams but also build credibility and trust within your community.

Give Back to the Community

As entrepreneurs, it's essential to use our success as a platform to give back to the community. Whether through charitable donations, volunteer work, or mentorship programs, leveraging our success to make a positive impact can be incredibly rewarding. By giving back, we not only contribute to the betterment of society but also strengthen our connection to the community and build a reputation as socially responsible business leaders.

Plan for Future Successes

While celebrating our current achievements is important, it's equally essential to plan for future successes. Setting new goals and objectives keeps us focused, motivated and continuously striving for growth and improvement. Whether it's expanding into new markets, launching innovative products, or achieving higher revenue targets, setting ambitious yet achievable goals ensures that we continue to push the boundaries of success and drive our businesses forward.

Conclusion

As we draw to a close, let's reflect on the journey we went on together—a journey fueled by hope, hustle, and transformation. Throughout this book, we have explored the power of dreams to inspire and drive us forward and the importance of taking tangible action to turn those dreams into reality. From my own experiences growing up in Monrovia to facing the complexities of the financial world, I have witnessed firsthand the transformative power of perseverance and determination. But beyond my personal journey lies a broader narrative—one that speaks to the universal truth that financial literacy and entrepreneurial spirit can empower individuals to achieve their dreams.

In the chapters that followed, we delved into the changing landscape of finance and employment, exploring how traditional careers are evolving into entrepreneurial ventures and the importance of upskilling and reskilling in today's job market. We have examined the shifting dynamics of employment and entrepreneurship, offering practical insights and strategies for those seeking to navigate this new terrain. From finding the right business idea to overcoming challenges and failures, we have explored the mindset and skills needed to thrive in the modern economy.

But perhaps most importantly, this book has been a celebration of hope—the unwavering belief that a better future is possible and that our dreams are within reach. It's a reminder that no matter how daunting the challenges may seem, with courage, confidence, and resilience, we can overcome any obstacle that stands in our way. It's a call to action for dreamers and doers alike to embrace failure as a stepping stone to success, to believe in themselves, and to never give up on their dreams.

As we part ways, I hope that the stories shared and lessons learned within these pages will continue to inspire and motivate you on your own journey of hope, hustle, and transformation. Remember, the path to success is not always easy, but with perseverance and determination, anything is possible. So go forth, dream boldly, and let the journey of hope, hustle, and transformation lead you to the life you have always imagined.

www.ingramcontent.com/pod-product-compliance
Lightning Source LLC
Chambersburg PA
CBHW051948150726
47999CB00004B/1300